BALLOONS OVER BEIJING

CAROL SUMNER KRECHMAN

ISBN: 979-8-89419-280-2 (sc)
ISBN: 979-8-89419-281-9 (hc)
ISBN: 979-8-89419-282-6 (e)

Because of the dynamic nature of the Internet, any web addresses or links contained in this book may have changed since publication and may no longer be valid. The views expressed in this work are solely those of the author and do not necessarily reflect the views of the publisher, and the publisher hereby disclaims any responsibility for them.

THE EWINGS
PUBLISHING

One Galleria Blvd., Suite 1900, Metairie, LA 70001
(504) 702-6708

FADE IN:

EXT. LOS ANGELES, CA - DAY

AERIAL VIEW: SANTA MONICA FREEWAY

A beat-up old VW van with balloons hanging out the back weaves in and out of traffic as it heads toward the downtown interchange. The convention center sign is overhead as the van exits the freeway.

EXT. LOS ANGELES CONVENTION CENTER - DAY

We follow the van to the loading dock of the Los Angeles Convention Center where it screeches to a halt. The sign on the van reads: ALICE'S WONDERLAND BALLOON FANTASIES.

ALICE SPRINGER (42), blonde, attractive, and energetic, exits in a frenzy. She checks her appearance in the side view mirror. She's not happy with what she sees, but in less than a minute, this disheveled, windblown woman has turned herself into the breezy model of corporate perfection. She pulls the balloons out of the back of the van and heads for the entrance.

INT. LOS ANGELES CONVENTION CENTER - DAY

POV - ALICE

A banner proclaims "Barron Industries
Welcomes First Annual Chinese-American
Trade Fair, April 1-5, 1989."

ELECTRICIANS string lights, and WORKERS
prepare balloon arches and bouquets under the
direction of SUSAN (25), Alice's assistant,
an off-the-wall, out-of-work actress.
Alice heads toward Susan. As she goes, she
checks items off on her clipboard.

                    ALICE
          (giving balloons to Susan)
        Here, use these. Some
        leftovers from yesterday's bar
        mitzvah.
                    (beat)
                    (whisper)
        Did the money come? We have
        to pay...

Before Susan can answer, something grabs
Alice's legs. Susan tries to steady her,
but she lands in a heap of balloons and a
tangle of pigtails and stubby legs.

TING (8), a pigtailed Chinese girl in a
Disneyland tee-shirt, is pulling on the
balloons and hugging Alice as she laughs
and shrieks in Chinese.

                    ALICE
         What the...

Susan tries to unwind Alice from the pile
as MINISTER HAX XUE WEN (70), the Head of
the Ministry of Mining, distinguished,
worldly and yet self-effacing, and MR. PING
XIAO LIU (40), Vice President of Barron
Industries, lean, tall, and Westernized
in his double-breasted pinstriped suit,
approaches.

Xiao Liu helps Alice up — balloons and
all — as Minister Han picks up Ting and
comforts her.
Alice waves Susan off.
Susan goes back to her work.

                  XIAO LIU
             (in a British accent)
         Are you hurt?

                   ALICE
         Only my pride.

                  XIAO LIU
         Well, let me help you.

He gathers up her papers, hands them to
her, and brushes off the back of her skirt.
They exchange a glance.

Alice is intrigued, and there's chemistry between them, but Ting's CRYING disrupts the moment.

                    MINISTER HAN
          Forgive my grandchild, miss.
          She is quite excited by the
          balloons. We have none in
          China.

Alice pats Ting on the head and smiles at her.
Ting clings to Alice.

                    ALICE
          You don't?

She stops. Her entrepreneurial mind is working. Alice offers Ting the balloons, but the child is suddenly shy and hides behind her grandfather's legs.

Suddenly Ting grabs the balloons and starts to run around the tables with them.
A BODYGUARD follows.
Alice and Xiao Liu laugh at Ting's antics.

                    ALICE
          Your granddaughter loves
          those balloons. Too bad your
          country doesn't have any.

DR. AARON BARRON, a portly, red-faced, and imperious 70-year-old tycoon, approaches.

Xiao Liu springs to attention.

                    MINISTER HAN
          If we had them, my
          granddaughter would...

                    DR. BARRON
                    (interrupting)
          Minister Han. How nice to see
          you again.

Dr. Barron grabs Minister Han's hand and
pumps it vigorously.
Minister Han shrugs at Alice then turns
his attention to Barron.

                    MINISTER HAN
          Yes, very nice. The fair
          hasn't begun, and I've already
          discovered a new product.

Alice puts out her hand to Dr. Barron.

                    ALICE
          Dr. Barron! I'm Alice
          Springer.

Dr. Barron ignores her, gives her a
patronizing glance, then turns to Xiao Liu.
Alice, embarrassed and a bit intimidated,
pulls her hand back.
Xiao Liu smiles at her in amusement.

                    ALICE
          You know, Alice's Wonderland
          Balloon Fantasies. Your
          company hired me to decorate
          tonight.

                    XIAO LIU
          I hired you. You came highly
          recommended.

Taken in by the flattery, she gives him an
appreciative look.

                    ALICE
          You won't be disappointed.

                    MINISTER HAN
          Your balloons are as nice as
          you are.

Dr. Barron, oblivious to Alice, tugs on
Minister Han's arm, almost pulling him
physically away from her.

                    BARRON
          Come, my friend, let's spend
          some time together before
          tonight's interviews. We must
          talk about the gold mines.

Alice does not want to let this opportunity
slip by.

                    ALICE
          I hope to see you again,
          Minister Han.

The minister is reluctant to leave, but Dr.
Barron is quite insistent.
Alice gives Barron a resigned look.

                  MINISTER HAN
          Goodbye, miss. I hope to see
          you tonight at the banquet.

Barron leads Han to a table at the back of
the convention center.
Xiao Liu, Ting, and the bodyguard follow.

INT. LOS ANGELES CONVENTION CENTER - NIGHT

The room has been transformed. It's an
extravaganza! Balloons, lights, drama, and
a big band plays as an emcee greets people.

Chinese and American DIGNITARIES, Minister
Han, and Dr. Barron sit on the stage at the
head table.

REPORTERS are gathered around Dr. Barron
and Minister Han. Several hundred people
fill the room.

INT. LOS ANGELES CONVENTION CENTER -
BACKSTAGE - NIGHT

Xiao Liu and Alice are talking as she
adjusts the lights.

                    XIAO
          Minister Han wants you to sit
          next to him at dinner, but
          let me warn you — Chinese men
          are known to be charmers.

She gives him a knowing glance.

                    ALICE
          I've learned that already.

INT. LOS ANGELES CONVENTION CENTER - STAGE,
HEAD TABLE - NIGHT

Its large banquet table set with Chinese
dishes, teapots, etc.

Minister Han stands to greet Alice.
Two REPORTERS throw a barrage of questions
at Dr. Barron.

Xiao Liu sits at Barron's side, fielding
questions and sparring with reporters.

                    REPORTER 1
          What's happening to the
          Chinese-American gold mine
          deal?

                    REPORTER 2
The rumors are this venture
will never get off the
ground.

                    REPORTER 1
Wall Street is waiting. Will
the contract be signed at
this trade fair?

                    XIAO LIU
Your question would better be
answered by Minister Han.

Minister Han is totally engrossed with
Alice and ignores the reporters.

                    REPORTER 1
Minister Han! What's the
progress of the negotiation?
The American public is
waiting.

                    MINISTER HAN
In China, we have a saying:
"The ox moves slow, but the
earth is patient."

He turns toward Alice, lifts the teapot,
and starts to pour her some tea.

                    MINISTER HAN
                        (beat)
Please.

She takes the teapot from his hand and pours his tea then starts to sip hers.

Minister Han turns to the reporters.

> MINISTER HAN
> As China's Minister of Mining,
> I know that gold is the best
> hedge against inflation...

He folds his hands gently on the table and continues.

> MINISTER HAN
> (continuing)
> Dr. Barron has impressed
> upon me the urgency. When we
> conclude our negotiation, you
> will know. We plan to—

> DR. BARRON
> (interrupting)
> We are very close to an
> agreement on this historic
> joint venture.

The reporters try to get Han's attention again, but he looks happy to let Barron and Xiao Liu do the talking. They write a few notes and then leave.

Minister Han turns toward Alice and lays on the charm.

Dr. Barron gets up and approaches the podium to speak. The band strikes a welcoming note.

At that moment, a thousand balloons are released from above the convention center and float to the floor. The audience begins to applaud.
Alice smiles brilliantly.

Dr. Barron waits patiently at the podium to begin his speech.

Alice and Xiao Liu exchange a glance. He lifts his glass to her nods.
Han is applauding.

                    MINISTER HAN
          How beautiful! Chinese people
          will love your balloons.

IN THE B.G., reporters, photographers, and TV crews are milling.

EXT. ALICE'S HANCOCK PARK HOUSE - NIGHT

With her shoes and jacket in hand, Alice approaches the large carved doors of this once-grand mansion.

She fumbles with her keys as she begins to open the door, but it is stuck. After much effort, she pushes it open. A ROSSINI OVERTURE BLASTS.

INT. ALICE'S HANCOCK PARK HOUSE - NIGHT

The hall is cluttered with the flotsam and jetsam of three teenagers. We also see several large pieces of sculpture in the hall as Alice throws her jacket over the arm of one and puts her shoes on another.

She picks up a stack of mail including bills, magazines, and a book.

CLOSE ON A WALL OF FAMILY PHOTOS:

Alice with twins (boy and girl) at different ages and Alice and Dave's wedding photo (a late '70s counterculture event).

Alice heads for the kitchen.

INT. ALICE'S HANCOCK PARK HOUSE - KITCHEN - NIGHT

DAVE (38), Alice's husband (bearded, lanky, with an earring and ponytail), is sitting on the floor by the sink, working on the garbage disposal. A boom box (the source of the Rossini) and a big shaggy dog (EINSTEIN) sit next to him. Tools are scattered around him. He turns down the music and gets up as he sees Alice come in.

                    DAVE
          Hi, honey. How'd it go today?
          Did my designs work OK?

She playfully traps him between her hips and the sink counter.

                    DAVE
              (warming up)
        Better not play around with
        the hired help. Is this what
        you did with the plumber?

                    ALICE
        I had to do something. We
        never paid him.

She drops the mail on the table, sits down, and opens the bills. She looks at them one by one.

                    ALICE
              (to herself)
        Gas company...
                 (she opens another)
        Water bill...
                    (another)
        Phone bill...
                    (beat)
        Did you ever think of going
        to China?

Einstein gives Dave a wrench. He adjusts a pipe, turns on the disposal, but nothing happens.

                    DAVE
        What?

                    ALICE
         We could take a second
         honeymoon, sell balloons to
         every Chinaman, and make
         millions!

                    DAVE
         Dreamer!

He puts the plunger handle to into the
drain and pushes it from side to side.
She opens the book. It's from the Planetary
Society.

                    ALICE
         *The Cosmic Cure to a World
         in Chaos?* Thirty bucks! Were
         broke, and you're ordering
         this?

He turns up the MUSIC slightly.

She look miffed and concerned as she opens
another envelope and takes out an official-
looking paper.

              CLOSE ON PAPER:

It's a notice from the bank warning that
foreclosure proceedings will begin in 30
days if her account is not current.

She gets up and starts to pace around the
kitchen.

                    ALICE
                 (determinedly)
        It's not going to happen. I
        won't let them take my house!

Dave, oblivious to Alice's trauma, turns
on the water and hits the disposal switch.
Nothing happens. He turns off the water,
and the handle comes off.

                    DAVE
        Who want this house? I'll pay
        someone to take it!

                    ALICE
        No one's going to take my
        house. Your psychic says
        I have the power to make
        anything happen.

                    DAVE
        Then, great magic one...come
        focus your power into this
        garbage disposal —

Alice humors him and walks to the sink.
She holds her hands over it. Alice stares
at her hands in amazement.

                    ALICE
        It worked! I do have power. I
        can make anything happen.

                    DAVE
          Then sell my sculpture to
          your Chinamen.

She picks up the bills and waves them at him.

                    ALICE
          I'm tired of living on the
          edge. China could be our
          way out. And now with your
          daughter here, there's another
          mouth to feed.

                    DAVE
          Why don't you get a real job!

                    DAVE
          Go back into the business
          world? No way. I'm not going
          to be your success object. My
          sculpture is my work.

He starts to cough.

                    DAVE
          And you knew it when you
          married me. Unless you were
          blinded by lust for
                    (cough)
          my body.

                    ALICE
          Yeh, that's when you had a
          body and I was Superwoman.

Alice gives him a resigned look as she
leaves the kitchen.
Dave pats Einstein and scratches his ears.

We hear Alice stumbling and swearing
off-screen.

                    ALICE
          Tomorrow you can fix this
          carpet.

                    DAVE
          Well, since you're going to
          China, get some Oriental rugs.

A door slams, and we hear loud ROCK MUSIC
off-screen.

INT. ALICE'S BATHROOM - NIGHT

It's the bathroom of a formerly affluent
woman with an old-fashioned tub, pink
monogrammed towel, a mirrored table with
fine perfume bottles on a tray.

Alice pours gel into the tub as she turns
on the water.
She undresses and pours an oil treatment
on her hair and runs her fingers through
it. She examines each pore in the mirror as
she wraps her hair in a towel.

She steps into the tub. The water's scalding hot.

                    ALICE
          Ehh! Shit.
                    (louder)
          Shit!

She grabs a towel, jumps out of the tub, and rushes out of the bathroom, dripping water as she goes.

The volume of the ROCK MUSIC increases as she opens the door.

INT. HALL - NIGHT

                    ALICE
               (yelling)
          Damnit! Turn off that water!

A door opens. TODD (20), Alice's son and an insufferable preppy, is on the phone with his hand over the mouthpiece.

                    TODD
          Mother, control yourself!
          Courtney's on the phone.
          She'll think we have no
          class.

He glares at Alice then closes his door.

Alice resumes her diatribe.

                    ALICE
          Dave. Do you hear me? Turn
          off the water!

She scowls and turns to the closed door
opposite. She bangs on the door, and it
opens.

DAWN (15), Dave's "punker" daughter, stands
there, looking blankly at Alice.
There's a horrible increase in the decibel
level of the music.

                    ALICE
          Turn down that awful music.

Dawn gives Alice a dirty look.

                    DAWN
          Yeh!

She shrugs, crosses the room, and turns off
the music as Alice is still screaming.

                    ALICE
          Turn it off!

                    DAVE (O.S.)
          Are you talking to me?

                    ALICE
          Yes! Turn off the cold water!

                    DAVE (O.S.)
          OK. I was only testing the
          drain.

Alice looks as if her life is out control.
She stomps her wet feet back toward the
bathroom.

INT. ALICE'S BATHROOM - NIGHT

Alice turns on the water again, and we
hear a loud knocking from the pipes as
brown water spurts out the faucet and into
the tub.

Alice slumps down on the closed toilet seat
and pounds her fists on the tub as she
bends over in total frustration.

INT. ALICE'S HANCOCK PARK HOUSE - MASTER
BEDROOM - MORNING

Einstein lies at the foot of their bed as
Alice and Dave make love. She screams in
delight.

The TV is on — morning news, no volume.
Dave nibbles Alice's ear.

                    DAVE
          Mmmm. You're good.

He continues his gentle caressing as Alice rubs his back.

                    ALICE
          Oh!

                    DAVE
          What's wrong? Did I hurt you?

She sits up.

                    ALICE
          It's me! I'm on TV!

               CLOSE ON TV:

                    ALICE
          It's the trade fair.

Alice turns up the VOLUME, and Dave looks at the screen.

               ANNOUNCER (V.O.)

The Chinese Minister will conclude his business in California and will return to China on Friday.

                    ALICE
          I look fat.

                    DAVE
          No, you look terrific, honey.
          A new star.

Dave nuzzles her neck, tries to take the remote control away from her.
Alice keeps the remote control out of his reach and INCREASES the VOLUME.

                    ANNOUNCER (V.O)
          Dr. Barron hopes the
          negotiations for the gold
          project will be concluded by
          that time.

Dave gets up and heads toward the bathroom. Einstein follows.

Alice finds herself on another channel and moves to the end of the bed in rapt attention. She's loving herself on the tube.

                    ALICE
          (calling out to Dave)
          I'm on channel 7 too!

There's no response from Dave.

Alice watches herself for a moment. She looks toward the bathroom and turns off the TV.

INT. MASTER BATHROOM - DAY

As Alice enters, she sees Dave holding the toilet handle, waving it at her.

                    DAVE
This damn house is falling
apart. Now I'll have to spend
the whole day fixing the
toilet.

                    ALICE
Our finances are in the
toilet too.

                    DAVE
Sell the house.

                    ALICE
Sell it! What's to sell? I've
used it for security on my
business ventures.

                    DAVE
              (superior)
Security comes from within.

                    ALICE
That's really helpful.

                    DAVE
So? We'll move to the beach.

                    ALICE
Right, we'll join the homeless
and camp out.

She rummages in a drawer, finds her hair
brush.

                    ALICE
          (brushing her hair furiously)
          Never mind, I'll make a deal
          with China.

She looks in the mirror and continues to
brush her hair.

                    DAVE
          Just what you need — more
          stress in your life.
                    (beat)
          Then we'll never make love.
                    (beat)
          What do you want for dinner?

She puts down the brush, turns, and looks
at him.

                    ALICE
          Chinese chicken salad on a
          bed of greens...thousand-
          dollar greens!

She heads for the door.

Dave looks at her back and sighs. He sits
down on the floor and hugs the dog as
Alice leaves.

                    DAVE
          Einstein, you're the only one
          I can trust. I know you won't
          turn on me.

EXT. HANCOCK PARK HOUSE - DAY

Alice heads for her car.
Dave, in bathrobe, waits as Einstein brings
him the newspaper from the end of the
driveway.

Alice gets in her car and starts the motor.
It SPUTTERS and belches smoke. The NOISES
get louder as Alice gets out of the car.
She lifts the hood and looks inside. The
car SPUTTERS, shakes, belches smoke, and
dies.

Dave sticks his head under the hood with
her. She pulls a wire from the ignition,
touches it to the battery cap, and the
motor turns over. Dave is amazed.

                    ALICE
          Works every time.

Alice's twins, Todd and JULIE, a "Deadhead"
in tie-dye and Birkenstocks, burst out of
the front door, arguing.

                    TODD
          Ma! She wore my sweater to
          a Dead concert, and now it
          smells like shit.

                    JULIE
          And "Old Spice" smells better?

                    ALICE
          Give it up! Drop your sweater
          at the cleaners on the way to
          the market.

She gets in, reaches over to the passenger
seat, lifts up a canvas bag, then holds it
out the window.

Dave takes the bag, looks inside, and pulls
out a piece of sculpture. It's a three-foot-
high very-well-done contemporary statue of
a nude woman.

Alice puts the car in reverse and sticks
her head out the window.

                    ALICE
          Don't forget to call the
          gallery today about your
          show.

The car sputters. She pulls out of the
driveway and lurches down the street as
Dave stands there, hugging his "statue
woman."

EXT. HANCOCK PARK BANK READY TELLER
MACHINE - DAY

Alice is at the ATM punching in numbers.
She makes a deposit. She waits. She takes
her receipt then punches more numbers.

A message appears on the screen:
"Please see Branch Manager. Insufficient
funds - Card Cancelled."

She looks down for her card. It hasn't
returned.
Now she's mad. She pushes more buttons.
Nothing happens. She pounds the machine
and kicks it in frustration.

CUT TO:

INT. ALICE OFFICE- DAY

The office is small and cluttered. It's in
the back of a balloon store. Susan is at her
desk, making a phone call. She looks up as
Alice enters, carrying a carton of balloons.

                    SUSAN
          I was just trying to get you.
          You've got a problem.

She points to the MAN (20s) and the WOMAN (late 30s) both dressed in grey suits with stern looks on their faces standing behind Alice by the front door.

                    SUSAN
                 (continuing)
         They say they're from the IRS.

                    ALICE
         I'm Alice Springer. Did you
         want to see me?

                 WOMAN AGENT
         We're here to see all your
         books and records. Didn't you
         get our notice?

                    ALICE
         No, I didn't, and I don't have
         any time right now, so you
         need to leave.

She opens the front door and indicates the way out.
The agents are stunned and make no move toward the door.

                    ALICE
         You'll have to call for an
         appointment if you want my
         time.

She take the woman's arm and escorts her
out the door. The man follows. She closes
the door and locks it behind them and
turns to Susan.

                    SUSAN
          Wow! What was that all about?

                    ALICE
          Call the accountant. Let her
          take care of it.
                    (beat)
          There never seems to be
          enough money.

                    SUSAN
          You have enough to cover my
          paycheck, don't you?

Alice thumbs through her Rolodex then
pushes a button on her speaker phone.
Before she can dial, there's an incoming
call.

                    MALE VOICE
               (with heavy breathing)
          Hello? Alice? Balloon
          Fantasies? I want to order an
          inflatable woman...
               (more heavy breathing)

Alice turns off the phone.

                    ALICE
          He's looking for his own brand
          of safe sex.

                    SUSAN
          Things are tough out in the
          single world.

Alice laughs and gives her a knowing glance.
It's apparent they're very close.

                    ALICE
          Hey! I got an idea from that
          call.

                    SUSAN
                 (disgusted)
          You're not going to sell
          inflatable women, are you?
          Things aren't that bad.

                    ALICE
          No. I'm thinking about safe
          sex and designer condoms.

                    SUSAN
          Condoms? That's been done
          already.

                    ALICE
          Not...flavored ones.

                    SUSAN
          Flavored! Yeh! For the man
          you love to lick!

They're both laughing hysterically.

                    ALICE
          Don't laugh. This could be a
          fast in and out business.

She's on a roll. Susan is still laughing as
she pictures an ad.

                    ALICE
                 (continuing)
          How about lemon zest? Put a
          little zest in your sex.

                                        CUT TO:

          And this is the last support
          check.

                    ALICE
          You're cutting them off three
          months before graduation?
          What a dad!

Harold ignores her last statement and heads
for the door.

                    HAROLD
          Why don't you let that artist
          husband of yours paint my
          house?

                    ALICE
          Your house? It's my house
          now. Get the hell out of
          here! And...
                    (beat)
          get a better rug!

He smiles disdainfully, as if to say "grow
up." Then he leaves.

                    SUSAN
          I can't see you ever married
          to that jerk.

                    ALICE
          That was another time.

                    SUSAN
          Dave's so mellow, and his
          balloon designs are awesome.

                    ALICE
          And he's so supportive...
                    (beat)
          but now I look at Harold's
          money, and I...
                    (beat)
          no... I couldn't have
          survived it.

Alice picks up the phone with determination and dials.

> ALICE
> (continuing)
> I'll do it myself!

She waits for someone to answer.

Susan gets two cups of coffee and gives one to Alice.
Alice gets a response.

> ALICE
> Mr. Xiao Liu Ping please.

She waits, drinks her coffee, and doodles "China – China - China" on a pad.

> ALICE
> Hello. This is Alice
> Springer. Yes
> (beat)
> I'd like your input about a
> business idea.

Susan gets up and gathers her things.

She waves at Susan "Don't leave." Susan sits down.

> ALICE
> (continuing)
> Monday? That will be fine.

                    (beat)
          Lunch! That would be great.
                    (beat)
          And do you think I could have
          five minutes of Dr. Barron's
          time?

Susan waits and doodles dollar signs on a
pad while Alice finishes the call.

                    ALICE
                 (continuing)
          I understand. I know he's a
          very busy man.
                    (beat)
          Well, you have a nice weekend
          too. Goodbye.

She hangs up the phone.

                    SUSAN
          What's so important?

                    ALICE
          That, my dear friend is a way
          to take the IRS off my back
          and get me to China.

The door opens. Julie bounds into the office.

                    JULIE
          Did you say China? The Dead
          are gonna have a concert on
          the Great Wall this summer.

She takes some papers off Alice's desk.

                    ALICE
          The Dead, the Dead. That's
          all you ever think about.

Alice gives Julie a disapproving look as
she gets up and tucks her daughter's shirt
into the back of her skirt.

                    ALICE
          I told you not to dress that
          way in my office.

                    JULIE
          You're always criticizing me...
          always judging me...always
          telling me what to do. I'm
          sick of it!

                    ALICE
          I only want what's best for you.
                    (beat)
          You'd look so much better with
          some lipstick and eye makeup.

                    JULIE
          And pay the animal killers?

                    ALICE
          No matter what I say, I'm
          wrong. Don't you see that
          I love you and I'm only
          thinking about your future?

                    SUSAN
          Well, my future's in the
          theater...

She's out door before Alice can say
anything.
                    (beat)
Alice glances at the door in disgust, but
gets right back to Julie.

                    ALICE
          There's so much you can
          do! You're bright, you're
          beautiful, and you have no
          financial responsibilities.

                    JULIE
          I'm not you, Mother. Leave me
          alone. I'm doing what I want
          to do.

                    ALICE
          If only I was your age, I
          would do it differently.

                    JULIE
          You still can.

Julie hit a nerve. Tears start to well up
in Alice's eyes.

                    ALICE
          There's not enough time. There
          never was enough time. I just

keep spinning my wheels, and
it seems like I'm stuck.

                JULIE
Well, that's you. Don't try to
change me.

                ALICE
I'm not. I don't expect you
to be Superman. I know that
doesn't work.

                JULIE
Oh, Mom....I know being both
a mother and a father hasn't
been easy.

                ALICE
But I still dream about
making a difference in this
world.

                JULIE
You've done more than any of
my friends' moms.

                ALICE
If only I can go to China.

                JULIE
And introduce balloons to
Chinese children. Maybe then
will you get off my case?

                    ALICE
          I'll try.
                    (beat)
          But for now, will you put on
          a little lipstick...please?

Julie laughs and gives her mother a hug.

Alice returns to her desk, and Julie goes
to the computer. She attaches earphones to
her head and begins the bookkeeping.

                                   CUT TO:

EXT. BARRON INDUSTRIES, DOWNTOWN LOS
ANGELES - DAY

Alice is on the street. She looks up to
check the address. She enters the building.

INT. DR. BARRON'S PENTHOUSE OFFICE - DAY

It's a finely appointed office. Dr. Barron,
Xiao Liu, and Vice Mayor Chen watch the
reception area on a closed-circuit TV.

POV - BARRON AND OTHERS

Behind a long marble counter, they see the
RECEPTIONIST, a formidable-looking woman
of 50+, and a SECURITY GUARD who wears a
uniform and holster.

The elevator opens. Alice jumps back as the door begins to close on her. It opens again, and she exits. She's frazzled as she heads for the receptionist.

The receptionist motions Alice to the end of the counter. Alice's hand shakes as she picks up a pen. She writes on a card and returns to the center of the counter, card in hand.

The receptionist motions Alice to sit on one of the couches in the spacious reception area.

                    DR. BARRON
          She'll be perfect! She's needy
          and naïve. She'll think we're
          doing her a favor.

He turns to Xiao Liu.

                    XIAO LIU
          She'll be an added inducement
          for Minister Han to approve
          our gold deal.

                    Dr. BARRON
          Let's bring her in.

Xiao Liu almost bows as he backs out
Barron's office door.

INT. RECEPTION AREA, DR. BARRON'S OFFICE - DAY

Alice sits on the couch. She's trying to read a magazine. She crosses then uncrosses her legs. She pulls her skirt down over her knees. She opens her purse, pulls out her compact, then examines her makeup in the mirror.

She does not see Xiao Liu approach.

                    XIAO LIU
          Miss Springer, how good to
          see you again.

As Alice stands up, the magazine and some papers fall to the floor. Flustered, she bends to retrieve them.

                    ALICE
          Sorry...

                    XIAO LIU
          Here...let me help.

He bends down. Their heads bumps. Both look at each other and laugh uncomfortably.

                    XIAO LIU
          Come, Dr. Barron's waiting.

He takes her arm. Alice looks startled but pulls herself together and confidently heads for Dr. Barron's office.

INT. DR. BARRON'S OFFICE - DAY

The door opens. Xiao Liu and Alice enter.

Barron stands behind his desk, smiles, and reaches out his hand to Alice.

                    Dr. BARRON
          It's easy to see why Minister
          Han Xue Wen was so taken
          with you.

Alice reaches across the desk and takes his hand. She shakes it enthusiastically. She's starry-eyed.

                    ALICE
          Oh, thank you. I never
          dreamed I'd be meeting with
          you today. I'm fascinated with
          China... I consider all this a
          wonderful opportunity.

Barron sits and motions her to the chair by the desk. She sits down.

                    ALICE
                  (continuing)
          Americans can learn so much
          from you. You've opened
          doors to so many countries...
          Russia...and now China.

                    DR. BARRON
          Well, you really know how to
          charm on old man.

She's not listening — just plowing forward.

                    ALICE
          Oh, if I could only spend a
          few weeks in China.

                    DR. BARRON
          Well, good because I have
          some business for you there.

She hasn't heard him.

                    ALICE
          First I'd go to Canton then
          Peking.

                    DR. BARRON
                 (emphatically)
          Miss Springer! I just said I
          want to send you to China.

                    ALICE
          You what?

                    DR. BARRON
          I am donating two mandrill
          monkeys to the Guangzhou Zoo,
          and I want your balloons
          there for the celebration.

Alice brightens. A COMMOTION is heard off-screen.

                    RECEPTIONIST (O.S.)
          You can't go in there!

The door opens.

Susan, dressed in red mandarin pajamas, stands there. She holds a large balloon bouquet with a banner attached. It says "Chinese-American Friendship." There are red, white, and blue-striped balloons and red balloons with gold stars in the arrangement.

Susan starts to SING to the tune of "God Bless America."

                    SUSAN
          God bless America, Red China
          too. We'll do business in
          friendship, Dr. Barron. It's
          all up to you!

                    DR. BARRON
          My goodness. What's this all
          about?

                    ALICE
          It's what I've been trying to
          tell you all morning. These
          balloons will make us a
          fortune in China.

                    DR. BARRON
          Us?

                    ALICE
          Yes, I came here for
          your backing. I want to
          manufacture balloons in
          China. There's two billion
          Chinese waiting for them.

                    DR. BARRON
          I've been accused of being
          full of hot air, my dear,
          but...balloons? Well, we'll see.

Dr. Barron stands and motions to Xiao Liu.

                    DR. BARRON
          Xiao Liu, take Miss Springer
          to lunch and explain all the
          details...and find out more
          about this balloon idea of
          hers.

Alice runs to Barron and kisses him. He's
taken aback.
She takes the balloon bouquet from Susan
and puts it on Barron's desk. She stands
back and admires it.

                    ALICE
          Now this makes a statement.

Barron looks pleased.

INT. BARRON INDUSTRIES EXECUTIVE DINING
ROOM — DAY

Alice and Xiao Liu linger over coffee. The
room is almost empty; lunch hour is long
over.

                    XIAO LIU
          Columbia. Funny, even though
          I left China 30 years ago,
          companies have always hired
          me as their China expert.

                    ALICE
          You really believe the
          Chinese are ready for
          balloons?

                    XIAO LIU
          I'm sure you will be a big
          success. All the children
          will love them.

                    ALICE
          I'd like to give you some for
          your children.

                    XIAO LIU
          I don't have any kids...I
          never married.

                    ALICE
      That's because you travel so
      much.

There's an awkward silence.

                    ALICE
                 (continuing)
      This will be the first time
      I'm away from my family.

                   XIAO LIU
      We'll be too busy for you to
      be lonely. You'll fall in love
      with China.

                    ALICE
      Pleases... I'm really busy...

                    DAWN
                 (a whisper)
      You don't like me. You don't
      like anything about me.

It looks as if Dawn may cry.

                    ALICE
      No, Dawn, what makes you —

                    DAWN
                (interrupting)
      I don't want to live in this
      house anyway! I'm gonna leave

tomorrow and go back to the
Ashram with my mom.

Alice stands and raises her hand to push
the bangs out of Dawn's eyes. Dawn, fearing
Alice is going to hit her, pulls back.

                    ALICE
          Hey, it's OK.

Dawn moves away then turns to look at Alice.

                    DAWN
          I heard you fighting with dad
          this morning.

                    ALICE
          Oh...
                    (beat)
          That was nothing... That's how
          we communicate.

                    DAWN
                    (holding back tears)
          I've never had my own room
          before.

Dawn is silent. She's looking at the floor.

                    ALICE
                    (smiles)
          Look, Dawn, I know this is a
          hard adjustment for you.

Dawn pushes her hair from her eyes.

                    DAWN
          My hair will grow out by the
          time you're back.

The music ends. We hear static. Dawn goes
to turn it off. She removes the tape and
gives it to Alice.

                    DAWN
          Promise me you'll take this
          tape to China.

                    ALICE
          OK. Maybe I'll even learn
          tai chi.

They both laugh. Maybe they'll be friends
after all.

                    ALICE
          Eat dinner. It's getting
          late. We'll talk more in the
          morning.

Dawn leaves.
Alice puts on the tape again and returns
to her desk and the map of CHINA.

INT. LIBRARY- LATER IN THE EVENING

Dave enters, carrying Alice's black lace
nightgown.

                    DAVE
          It's getting late. Come to
          bed, honey.

                    ALICE
          I don't want to come to bed
          now, but I want you to come
          to China with me.

                    DAVE
          How's running to China going
          to solve any of our problems?

He walks to the desk in disgust and throws
the nightgown on top of the magazines.

                    ALICE
          Your know Barron's giving
          me $5,000 plus, and all I
          have to do is deliver some
          monkeys and balloons for
          the children's festival in
          Beijing.

                    DAVE
          You're a mother, not a
          zookeeper.
                    (beat)
          What about the kids?

                    ALICE
          Kids? It feels more like a
          zoo around here!

Todd bursts onto the scene, almost
colliding with Alice.

                    TODD
          I've had it! Between the
          Grateful Dead and heavy
          metal, I can't stand it
          around here.

He confronts Dave and Alice.

                    TODD
                 (continuing)
          Your daughters are driving me
          nuts. A man has to have some
          privacy and peace and quiet.

Alice looks around.

                    ALICE
          Where's the man?

Todd's just warming up.

                    TODD
          Do something about this.
          Courtney won't set foot in
          this house. I want my own
          apartment.

                    ALICE
        If you're such a man, get a
        job and pay for it. There's
        the door!

                    TODD
        Me, what about him getting a
        job? He's got a free ride on
        my dad's back...

                    DAVE
        You little shit!

Dave grabs Todd by the neck and pushes him
into the wall. They fight, and it looks as
if they are about to kill each other.

                    ALICE
        Dave, let him go! Get out of
        here, Todd, now!

Todd stomps out.

                    ALICE
        I've just about had it with
        this marriage and this
        family. I'm going to China...

                    DAVE
        I don't want you to go. Who'll
        take care of the kids, the
        house, the plants?

She picks up the nightgown and throws it in Dave's face.

                    ALICE
          That's it, isn't it? I'm the
          breadwinner and mother and
          father around here. Well, I'm
          going, and you'd better get
          your act together. Otherwise,
          we're through!

She gathers her papers, the magazines, and some photos. She walks out the door and purposefully slams it behind her. The map of China floats off the wall.

                                        CUT TO:

VIEW OF BOEING 747 AIR CHINA FLYING ABOVE THE CLOUDS INTO THE SUN

INT. GUANZHOU AIRPORT - DAY

Alice emerges into a crowd of pushing, shoving commuters. Her baggage, including a monkey cage, is unloaded by TWO PORTERS.

She looks anxious and lost.

She asks several people for directions, but no one speaks English.

She waits, standing by the monkey cage, her luggage at her feet.
The mandrills are chattering and screeching as they swing all over the cage.
CHINESE PEOPLE gather around Alice and the cage. They laugh and point at the monkeys. Some imitate the animals. Alice looks helpless.

She turns and collides with Xiao Liu.

She throws her arms around him in relief. He gently pushes her away and starts to lead her through the crowd. She looks forlornly back at her luggage and the cage as Xiao Liu marches on. She follows him.

They meet Ting and her governess, JANE (40), an elegant, tall Chinese woman with a British accent.

                    XIAO LIU
          This is Jane Chung. She looks
          after Ting, and she'll help
          you while you are our guest.

Jane greets Alice warmly and motions to the DELEGATION OFFICIALS.
MINISTER TSO (50s), the Minister of Foreign Economic Relations and Trade (MOFERT), a short, slight and charming man in a Mao suit presents Alice with his business card as he shakes her hand.

                    JANE
          May I present Minister Tso,
          the Minister of Foreign
          Economic Relations and Trade,
          which we call MOFERT.

Alice fumbles in her purse and looks
embarrassed as she's introduced to
Minister Tso.

Jane motions toward other dignitaries.

VICE MAYOR CHEN (50), a dour-looking beefy
man in a military uniform, steps forward.

                    JANE
          And this is our Honorable
          Vice Mayor Chen. He is
          a famous hero of the
          revolution.

Alice searches the bottom of her purse.
She finds her business cards and hands a
crumpled one to Vice Mayor Chen as she turns
to face the others with her cards in hand.

                    ALICE
          I'm so honored to meet you,
          and it's such a thrill to at
          last be in China. This is a
          dream come...

Xiao Liu takes her by the arm and motions
to a porter to get her bag.

                    XIAO LIU
         Miss Springer, please, we
         must hurry.

He leads her away from the rest of the
delegation.
Ting breaks from the group and runs to
Alice. She shyly presents her with a
bouquet then grabs her around the legs.
Alice picks her up and hugs her warmly.

The procession, led by Xiao Liu, with Alice
carrying Ting, moves through immigration
and out of the airport. Alice's luggage and
the monkey cage on a dolly bring up the
rear.

                                        CUT TO:

INT. DONG FONG HOTEL, ALICE'S ROOM - DAY

It's an old elegant '50s-style room. There's
a carved teak bed and cabinets, satin
tufted bedspread, high ceilings, and a view
of the park partially blocked by a window-
mounted air conditioner.

Alice unpacks. Everything is very wrinkled.

She goes through the pockets of her
suitcase and finds her steamer and adaptor
kit. She fills the steamer with water from
a pitcher.

She crawls on the floor, trying different outlets. None fits. There's a knock on the door. The door opens. It's Xiao Liu.

                    XIAO LIU
          Oh, excuse me. Did I
          interrupt your exercise?

Alice, embarrassed, jumps up and almost knocks over the TV as the steamer flies out of her hands and spills all over Xiao Liu's pants.

                    ALICE
          Oh my god! I'm so sorry!

She runs into the bathroom and quickly returns with a towel.
She drops to her knees and starts to blot off his pants.
Xiao Liu pulls Alice to her feet.

                    XIAO LIU
          It's all right. They'll dry.
          Relax. Let's have some tea.

He goes to the tea set on the credenza and begins to prepare tea. Alice, regaining her composure, sits in a large chair by the window.

                    ALICE
          Looks like I've made a
          complete fool of myself, and

I've only been in China an
hour.

                    XIAO LIU
Chinese or American tea?
The Chinese will calm your
nerves.

                    ALICE
Will it cure a chronic klutz?

Xiao Liu looks at her and laughs.

                    ALICE
Oh, never mind. Chinese, of
course.
                    (beat)

She gets up and starts to pace around the
room.

                    ALICE
                    (continuing)
All this protocol is more
than I expected...and my
clothes are a wrinkled mess.
I still have to attend the
banquet, make my business
contacts, and I only have a
few weeks in China.

                    XIAO LIU
Relax. Drink you tea.

He hands her the cup.

Alices sits down.

                    XIAO LIU
                   (continuing)
          China and we have plenty of
          time. Now, let me tell you
          what to expect...

He sits down in a chair opposite her and
begins to drink his tea.

Alice sips her tea, sighs, and smiles in
gratitude at Xiao Liu.

                                    CUT TO:

INT. GUANGZHOU RESTAURANT - NIGHT

The banquet hall in this 2400-year-old
building overlooks a giant atrium filled
with orchids and other exotic flowers.

Alice is dazzled and overwhelmed by the
beauty. She's the center of attention as
she enters the room on Xiao Liu's arm.

                    ALICE
          Oh, Xiao Liu, I had no idea!
          I thought China was a poor
          country.

She grabs his hand in panic as she sees
the dignitaries line up to greet her.

                    XIAO LIU
                 (as an aside)
          Just remember to watch me,
          and you'll do fine.

He takes Alice by the arm, and they start
to walk down the line.
Alice shakes Vice Mayor Chen's hand. She
presents her business card and receives one
in return. She stops, looks at the card for
a moment, and smiles before she moves on.

Next, she meets FU SHAN (25), Vice Mayor
Chen's bodyguard, a tall, frozen-faced,
and sinister-looking man in a Chinese army
uniform. He whispers something in Xiao
Liu's ear and pulls him away.

Striking out independently, Alice greets
the other dignitaries one by one. She enjoys
herself as she chats and works the room.
Jane approaches and takes Alice aside.

                    JANE
                 (whisper)
          Excuse me. It is proper for
          everyone to wait for you to
          sit down before they are
          seated.

Alice looks anxiously around the room for
Xiao Liu.

                    ALICE
          Where's Xiao Liu? He was
          supposed to help me. Where do
          I sit?

                    JANE
          Follow me.

Jane leads Alice to a large round table
with fine china, full crystal service,
place cards, and ivory chopsticks.

Alice is seated next to Vice Mayor Chen and
Minister Tso from MOFERT.
Jane sits opposite Alice.

Jane introduces Alice to all at the table.

The vice mayor serves Alice. That is
tradition.

Alice serves the vice mayor. That is not
tradition.
All others at the table cover their mouths
and laugh.
Alice struggles with her chopsticks and
drops jellyfish in her lap.
One by one, as the different courses are
served, the dignitaries stand to propose
a toast in Chinese. Alice sips her drink,
chokes, then puts the glass down. The

Chinese indicate she is to finish the glass down, and not wanting to offend, she complies.

Each time the glasses are refilled, another toast is made, and all present lift their glasses, drink, and yell "*Ganbei.*" With each drink, Alice enjoys it more.

                    ALICE
          (tipsy and loose-tongued)
     You guys really know how to
     throw a party. The only thing
     missing is balloons.
          (beat)
     Lucky for you I'm going to
     open a balloon factory here.

At this announcement, Minister Tso turns in his chair.

                  MINISTER TSO
     Oh, really. You have contract
     with Chinese government? I
     thought you the monkey lady.

                    ALICE
     Oh, you speak English! I
     didn't...

The vice mayor stands, looks at Alice, raises his glass, and toasts in Chinese.

                    VICE MAYOR CHEN
                  (speaking in Chinese)
                Alice tries to continue
                her talk with Minister Tso,
                ignoring the vice mayor.

                         JANE
                  (from across the table)
                Alice, the vice mayor is
                proposing a toast to you and
                the monkeys.

                          ALL
                Ganbei!

Alice downs another glass and turns to
Minister Tso. She stands and raises her
glass that has been refilled by an ever-
attentive WAITER.

                         ALICE
                I'm more than a monkey lady.
                I'm a business lady.

She grabs on to the table for support as
she sits down again.

                         ALICE
                     (continuing)
                I'm a balloon lady. Here's to
                the balloon business!

She raises her glass and drinks again. All
eyes turn to her.

Xiao Liu returns from the patio, walks to her side, and leans over to talk to her.

> ALICE
> Where've you been? Do you
> know Minister Chen and Major
> Tso... I mean
> > (giggle)
> Mayor...

> XIAO LIU
> (whispering sternly)
> Protocol! Remember what we
> talked about. Everyone is
> waiting for your official
> toast to end the party.

Alice, confused about what she's to do, sits for a few moments while all eyes are on her again.

Slowly she gets to her feet and raises her glass. She weaves slightly, spills a bit of wine on the vice mayor's head, and grabs Xiao Liu for support.

> ALICE
> My Chinese friends, here's
> to you! And here's to the
> monkeys too! See you tomorrow
> at the zoo.
> Too-dol-loooodle-loo!

She slowly sinks down under the table.

Xiao Liu and Mayor Chen pick her up as the
assembled group put their hands over their
mouths and laugh.

EXT. GUANGZHOU RESTAURANT - NIGHT

Alice leans on Xiao Liu. She lurches, bends
over, and breathes deeply as if she may be
sick.

                    XIAO LIU
          I should have warned you
          about the *maotai*...it's potent.
          But I promise...you won't have
          a hangover in the morning.

Xiao Liu leaves to get the car as Alice
holds on to a column to keep from falling.

A crowd of young noisy people sit in the
outdoor cafe across the street.

                    FU SHAN
          You don't fit in here. You
          belong home with your family.

The car arrives. Alice bumps her head as
Xiao Liu and the DRIVER help her into the
back seat.

                    XIAO LIU
          Lie down, you'll feel better.
          We'll be at the hotel before
          you know it.

Alice has passed out in the back seat as
Xiao Liu starts to get into the front seat.
Mayor Chen approaches, yelling to XIAO LIU
in Chinese.
(English subtitles)

                    MAYOR CHEN
          Xiao Liu, wait! Hu Yaban's
          dead.

                    FU SHAN
          That's what all those students
          are talking about.

He gestures to the crowd across the street.

                    XIAO LIU
          You and your Red Guard ideas,
          always looking for trouble.

                    MAYOR CHEN
          This could be the start of a
          revolution.

                    FU SHAN
          My sister's a student at
          Beijing University, and
          they've begun to gather in
          Tiananmen Square.

                    XIAO LIU
          That has nothing to do with me.

MAYOR CHEN
The gold deal could be in
trouble, and even the monkeys
and the beautiful blonde may
not make a difference.

XIAO LIU
It's just politics. China
needs this deal.

FU SHAN
You and your Western mind.
You've forgotten that China
has survived without your
imperialist ways. A new wind
is blowing...mark my words.

XIAO LIU
Well, winds blow in both
directions, my friend.

Alice stirs and lifts her head.

ALICE
Xiao Liu, who's fighting?
What's going on?

XIAO LIU
It's nothing. We're leaving.

Xiao Liu looks annoyed as he turns to get
into the car.

                    MAYOR CHEN
              Just be careful, my friend.

Xiao Liu gets into the car, sits, and rolls
down the window as the car begins to pull
away from the curb.

                    XIAO LIU
              Friendship and revolution
              don't mix.

The car drives off.

                                          CUT TO:

INT. DONG FONG HOTEL - LATER IN THE EVENING

It's old China opulence with marble
columns, crystal chandeliers, gold leaf
carvings, and a high ornate ceiling.

Alice leans heavily on Xiao Liu. Her eyes
are closed as she staggers to the elevator
with him. She opens one eye.

At her hotel door, Xiao Liu holds her up
with one hand as he reaches into her purse
with the other. After much struggling, he
finds her key, opens the door, and helps
Alice inside.

INT. DONG FONG HOTEL, ALICE'S ROOM - ALMOST
DAWN

                    ALICE
          Oh...I feel sick... Just get me
          to my bed...

                    XIAO LIU
          A few more steps and...

As Alice starts to sit on the bed, she
feels an overwhelming urge. She covers her
mouth and runs to the bathroom.

We hear the water running as Alice is
coughing off-screen.
Xiao Liu pours some tea and leaves it on
her bedside table. He lets himself out of
the room.

Alice comes out of the bathroom and looks
around for Xiao Liu. She sees the tea. She
sits on the bed, puts her head down on her
hands, and cries.

She picks up the phone... It's dead.

She gets up, closes the drapes, and double
locks the door.

She returns to the bed, drinks her tea,
and tries the phone again. No luck. She
turns on her Walkman tape. We HEAR the
CHINESE MUSIC Dawn gave her as she leans
back on the bed.

CUT TO:

INT. HANCOCK PARK HOUSE, GARAGE
STUDIO - DAY

A copy of the same CHINESE MUSIC plays as
Dave works on his sculpture.

EXT. HANCOCK PARK HOUSE - SAME TIME

Four teenagers in leather jackets and on
motorcycles roar up the circular driveway.
One of the kids is Dawn.

The lead cycle skids, goes out of control,
and crashes through the bay window into
the studio.

INT. HANCOCK PARK HOUSE STUDIO - SAME TIME

The motorcycle crashes through the bay
window. It narrowly misses Dave but
shatters a piece of sculpture, which
showers Einstein.

STASH (18) lands in a heap of shattered
glass, wood, and plaster. He's dazed as
he climbs out of the mess. He's wearing a
black space-age motorcycle helmet; and as
he takes it off, we see a skinhead 6'4" boy
lumbering toward Dave.

                    DAVE
          Oh, shit...what the hell is
          going on here?

Dawn and the group run in the front door.

                    DAWN
              (running over to stash)
          Oh my god, Stash, are you
          hurt?

She has her arms around Stash.

                    DAVE
                 (angry)
            Is *he* hurt?

He grabs Dawn and pulls her off Stash.

Just then, Todd bolts into the studio as
Einstein shakes the dust off his fur.

                    TODD
              (brushing off his pants)
          These are my Polos, and
                    (beat)
          that was beveled glass! Who's
          gonna pay to fix it?

                    DAVE
          I'm calling the police.

                    TODD
          You can't do that...the
          scandal! Courtney will
          find out.

                    DAVE
          That's too bad.

                    DAWN
          Dad! These are my friends.

Julie, rubbing sleep from her eyes, enters
the studio. She saw the scene then rushes
over to Dawn.

                    JULIE
          Are you hurt? What happened?

                    DAWN
          I'm OK, but my dad has
          flipped out.

                    TODD
          Shut up, Julie!

                    DAVE
          Enough! I've had it. You go to
          your rooms!

He turns to Stash.

                    DAVE
                 (continues)
          You just stay here until the
          police come.

                    DAWN
          You can't talk to my friends
          like that.

                    TODD
          This isn't even your house!

Dave grabs Dawn and roughly pushes her
toward the door.
Stash starts after them.
Julie runs to Stash and tries to stop him.

Einstein positions himself between Dave and
Stash.

                    JULIE
          Stash...Don't mess with him...
          He's got his black belt.

Dave turns and assumes the attack position.
Stash keeps coming. Julie gets out of the
way. Dawn grabs and holds on to Stash.
Einstein's barking and trying to protect
Dave.

                    DAWN
          Stash, don't... Just do what
          he says.

Stash breaks loose, and he and Dave get
into a kickboxing match. Dave downs Stash.
Julie and Dawn pull him off Stash.

                    TODD
          Oh, great! This scene's right
          out of *Ninja Turtles*.

Julie gives her brother a dirty look as she
comforts Dawn.

                    DAVE
          Right. Those days are gone as
          of this moment.

                                        CUT TO:

INT. MAYOR CHEN'S LIMOUSINE - DAY

Fu Shan is sitting with the driver as Jane
and Alice sit in the back seat. Jane hands
Alice a jar of yellow liquid.

                    JANE
          I knew *maotai* would affect
          you, so I brought you
          something special.

Alice opens the jar, smells it, and smiles
in recognition.

                    ALICE
          It smells like Jewish
          penicillin.

Alice takes a sip.

                    ALICE
          And it tastes just like my
          mother's chicken soup.

                    JANE
          Warmth in the stomach clears
          your brain.

                    ALICE
          You sound like my mother. She
          always says, "Eat, eat, you'll
          feel better."

Alice finishes the soup.

                    ALICE
          Oh, what a fool I made of
          myself last night. I'm so
          embarrassed to see Xiao Liu.

The limo is at the entrance of the
Guangzhou Zoo. All the flags fly at half
staff.

                    JANE
          Xiao Liu has other things to
          think about. China's beloved
          prime minister has just died.

EXT. LIMO - GUANGZHOU ZOO - DAY

We follow the limo through the zoo until
it stops at the mandrill cage. Many young
CHINESE WORKERS are doing tai chi as Alice
and Jane approach. The limo stops, and
Alice and Jane get out. A WOMAN carrying a
clipboard greets them.

                    WOMAN
                (in Chinese)
          Welcome. My workers will be
          ready in a few minutes.

Jane translates, then Alice and Jane join
the tai chi.
IN THE B.G., Fu Shan observes the scene and
takes notes.

They finish, and Alice walks over to a
table by the workers and unfurls her
blueprints.

                    WOMAN
          (talks to the workers in Chinese)

                    JANE
                (to Alice)
          She's introducing you to the
          group and telling them of the
          importance of the day. You
          impressed them with your tai
          chi. They like you.

Alice smiles and nods at the workers and hands the foreman the blueprints.

Using gestures, she demonstrates how to operate the helium tank for all the workers. She ties a balloon to a grid and gestures that they do the same.

The work begins. Fu Shan furtively takes photos.

EXT. GUANGZHOU ZOO - LATER THAT DAY

Balloons arch in front of the cage with a banner hanging between. Balloon pagodas are on each side, topped by American and People's Republic of China (PRC) flags — one in red, white, and blue, the other in red and gold.

Ting, Jane, and Alice survey the scene. Alice is so happy. She hugs Ting and some of the workers.

Vice Mayor Chen approaches with Minister Tso and Fu Shan.
Alice turns to Jane and whispers.

                    ALICE
          Where's Xiao Liu? I need his
          help to sell Minister Tso.

Jane gives her an "I don't know" look as Mayor Chen takes Alice's hand.

                    MAYOR CHEN
          My zoo has never looked so
          beautiful. We are so happy
          you are here.

She shakes Mayor Chen's hand then turns to
face Minister Tso.

                    ALICE
          Now you know why I want
          a balloon factory in your
          country.

                    FU SHAN
          Our children have enough of
          your Western ideas.

Minister Tso gives him a look that "could
kill."

                    ALICE
          What's wrong with children
          having fun?

                    FU SHAN
          Children are the future of
          China. They learn nothing
          from balloons except to waste
          time.

                    ALICE
          You're making it sound like a
          political plot.

                    MINISTER TSO
          Balloons are not political,
          but a factory would be too
          costly.

Minister Tso takes Alice's arm and walks
her away from Fu Shan to the dais. Jane
and Vice Mayor Chen follow.

Fu Shan disappears into the crowd.

School children led by Ting parade into the
area. Each one is holding a balloon with the
imprint of an American Flag and Chinese Flag.

Alice smiles as the speeches begin. Local
TV and newspaper reporters are covering
the event. The mandrills run around their
cages as thousands of balloons fly into the
China sky. The crowd cheers and applauds.

The reporters crowd around Alice.

                                        CUT TO:

INT. GUANGZHOU OFFICE BUILDING - DAY

It's dark and dingy, vintage 1930s. Xiao Liu
talks to a CLERK at the reception counter.

                    XIAO LIU
          I'm looking for some gold
          mine records.

                    CLERK
         Yes, and who do you
         represent? You'll need
         permission to see files.

Xiao Liu hands some documents and a carton
of cigarettes to the clerk.

                   XIAO LIU
         I'm here under the authority
         of Minister Han Xue Wen.

The clerk examines the papers and puts the
cigarettes under the counter.

                    CLERK
         Oh, well, that's a different
         story. Follow me. I'll show
         you the files.

The clerk comes around the counter, and
Xiao Liu follows him down the hall and up
some stairs.

We follow as they enter a cluttered,
dark storage room. Several file cabinets
line the walls. There's a dusty table in
the center of the room. The clerk stops,
unlocks a drawer, and pulls out a file.

                    CLERK
         What you want is right here.
         Let me know when you're
         finished.

He hands the file to Xiao Liu and leaves
the room.
Xiao Liu goes through the papers, finds
what he's looking for, and spreads the
documents out on the table.

                                  CUT TO:

EXT. TRAIN STATIOM -DUSK:

A passenger train is waiting at the
platform between several high-rise
apartment buildings. TV antennas block the
sky, and laundry hangs from every balcony.

(NOTE: THE NEXT SCENE IS INTERCUT BETWEEN
DAVE AND ALICE ON THE PHONE)

Alice stands at a phone booth, talking.

IN THE B.G., Fu Shan talks to a conductor
and points at Alice. Then he gets on the
train. Alice doesn't see him.

                    ALICE
          I tried last night, but I
          couldn't get through. Did I
          wake you?

INT. DAVE'S STUDIO - NIGHT

He looks around at the mess.

                    DAVE
          Great, honey. Just great.

EXT. TRAIN STATION - DAY

                    ALICE
          I sent a FAX to Susan about
          everything. Give my love to
          train's leaving.

INT. DAVE'S STUDIO - DAY

                    DAVE
          Try to call again from
          Beijing. I love you.

EXT. TRAIN STATION - DAY

Alice hangs up the phone and heads for the
train.

INT. TRAIN COMPARTMENT - DUSK

Lace curtain cover the windows and lace
doilies cover the seats. Jane, Xiao Liu,

and Alice are sitting. Ting is on Jane's
lap, asleep.

                    ALICE
          Everyone loved the balloons
          except Fu Shan. What is it
          with him anyway?

                    XIAO LIU
          He's one of the old-time Red
          Guards.

Jane gives Xiao Liu a look that signals
"Enough, change the subject."

                    ALICE
          No wonder he made a political
          deal out of the balloons.

                    JANE
          The vice mayor was impressed
          with Alice's decoration, and
          the children were so excited.

                    XIAO LIU
          I'm sorry I missed that, but
          let's go to the dining car, and
          you can tell me all about it.

                    JANE
          You two go ahead. I'll stay
          and put Ting to bed.

INT. TRAIN PASSAGEWAY

The train is lurching as Xiao Liu and Alice
walk through the second-class cars. They
pass many passengers playing cards, eating
and drinking or sleeping

He holds onto her as the train goes around
a curve and she loses her balance.

INT. DINING CAR - DUSK

They enter the first- class dining car and
sit down opposite a CHINESE COUPLE.
Xiao Liu greets them in Chinese as they sit
down.
A WAITER stands by the table.

Xiao Liu speaks to the waiter in Chinese.

                    XIAO LIU
          These people are very curious
          to see a foreign woman
          traveling alone. I told them
          you were my wife

He laughs heartily.

                    ALICE
          I've never been a Chinese
          wife. How should I act,
          honorable Chinese husband?

                    XIAO LIU
                (still laughing)
        Just drink some plum wine,
        and it will come naturally
                    (beat)
        China is very seductive.

Alice considers her answer before speaking.

                    ALICE
        Yes
                    (beat)
        I think I know what you mean.
        I feel it creeping under my
        skin.

                    XIAO LIU
        Every time I return, my
        Chinese bones get caught up
        in the rhythm.

The train has stopped at a town. A GROUP OF
TEN SMALL CHILDREN enter the dining car,
selling candy. Alice buys a bag and gives
them balloons.

                    XIAO LIU
        How much did you pay for the
        candy?

                    ALICE
        I gave them one or two yuans
        each.

Xiao Liu jumps up and runs after the children. He speaks to them in Chinese and holds out his hand. The children each give him a coin. He returns to Alice.

                    ALICE
          What were you doing?

                  XIAO LIU
          Here...
              (he hands her the coins)
          We don't want our people to
          get corrupted.
          Hardliners like Mayor Chen
          and Fu Shan still have power.

                    ALICE
                 (laughing)
          But I bought the candy to
          corrupt you.

She hands the bag of candy to him, and he puts it in his pocket.

                  XIAO LIU
                 (laughing)
          It'll take more than a bag of
          candy.

The waiter appears.

Xiao Liu takes two glasses and a bottle of wine from the waiter. He cleans each glass with his napkin before he pours the wine.

He hands Alice her glass and lifts his in
a toast.

                    XIAO LIU
          To my new wife, the balloon
          princess.

                    ALICE
          Is polygamy still the custom
          in China?

                    XIAO LIU
          Three's the limit.

Alice and Xiao Liu laugh as they click
their glasses and drink.
The waiter reappears with two bowls of
noodles. He sets them down on the table in
front of Xiao Liu and Alice.

Xiao Liu takes Alice's chopstick and his
own and wipes them off with his napkin. He
hands Alice's back to her.

He picks up his bowl and chopstick and starts
to eat, slurping the noodles as he goes.

                    XIAO LIU
          Pick up the bowl and eat as
          I do.

Alice complies. We hear her slurping.

The waiter arrives with a whole fish. He
sets it down on the middle of the table.
At the same time, the other couple pay
their check and leave, nodding and smiling
at Xiao Liu and Alice as they go.

Xiao Liu takes some fish from the bones
and serves Alice then takes the head in
his chopsticks and eats it whole. Alice
stares at him as he chews on the fish head
— eyeballs and all.

Xiao Liu stops after swallowing an eyeball.

                    XIAO LIU
          Eating the head is a delicacy
          in China.

                    ALICE
          In my country, princesses
          never eat heads.

She laughs at her joke but stops dead to
watch a cockroach parade across the table.
She pushes her plate away.

There's an uncomfortable silence as Xiao
Liu continues eating.

                    ALICE
          It must have been very hard
          for you to leave Shanghai.

Xiao Liu pauses and looks out the train
window.
We see green fields plowed by oxen, great
mountains looming in the horizon as the
sun begins to set.

He turns to face Alice and sighs.

                    XIAO LIU
          I had no choice.
                    (beat)
          The Red guard attacked our
          bank, took our house, and I
          lived on the street until we
          could escape to Hong Kong.

                    ALICE
          What a terrible experience.

                    XIAO LIU
          We believe in the balance of
          the yin and yang. They both
          teach us a lesson.

                    ALICE
          Tell me more.

The lights dim in the train as it moves
through the night. Alice and Xiao Liu
continue talking.

INT. DAVE'S STUDIO HANCOCK PARK - DUSK

In the dim light, Dave and Julie sweep the shattered glass and broken sculpture from the floor.

                    JULIE
          I called and called China,
          but I can't find Mom.

                    DAVE
          I know you want to talk with
          her. I miss her too.

                    JULIE
          Maybe it's better that she
          doesn't know. We got to get
          this fixed before she gets
          home.

                    DAVE
          Your mom told me I have to
          take responsibility. This
          must be it.

                    JULIE
          We'll get it done together.

                    DAVE
          Thanks, and maybe there's
          more you can help me with. I
          don't understand Dawn.

                    JULIE
          I'll try.
                    (beat)
          Don't worry. Mom doesn't
          understand me either.

                                        CUT TO:

INT. TRAIN PASSAGEWAY - DAY

The train has stopped and two PEOPLE'S
LIBERATION ARMY (PLA) OFFICERS knock on the
door to the compartment. Alice is nervous
as they open the door, barking orders in
Chinese.

                    ALICE
          What's going on?

                    JANE
          It's just routine. They want
          to see our papers.

                    ALICE
          But why? We haven't don't
          anything.

                    XIAO LIU
                    (annoyed)
          They're checking everyone's
          papers.
                    (beat)
          Provincial peasants!

Alice, Jane, and Xiao Liu present their
papers.
The officers nod.
Everything seems to be in order when one
of the soldiers notices a helium tank on
the floor.

                    SOLDIER #1
        (in Chinese with English subtitles)
              What is that?

He bends over and pulls out the tank
while his partner looks under the seat,
discovering two more.

                    Alice
                (to Xiao Liu)
          What do they want with my
          tanks.

Xiao Liu and the officers have a heated
conversation in Chinese.

                    XIAO LIU
            (to Alice, disgusted)
          Bureaucrats! They think you
          are an American student and
          that the tanks are bombs.

                    ALICE
          Tell them they're just filled
          with air. Let me show them.

She grabs for a tank, but the soldier isn't cooperating. A tug-of-war begins.

                    ALICE
          Xiao Liu, say something!
          Help me.

Xiao Liu sweet-talks the officer, who reluctantly lets Alice have the tank.

As Alice sets the pressure gauge, the soldiers jump back and pull out their revolvers. They've mistaken the regulator for a handgun.

Xiao Liu jumps in front of Alice to shield her, yelling in Chinese at the PLA officers.

                   XIAO LIU
          (in Chinese with English subtitles)
             Put down your guns! That's
             her regulator for the tanks.

Alice drops the regulator and puts up her hands.

                    ALICE
          Don't shoot, don't shoot. I'm
          innocent.

The officer picks up the regulator, looks at it, then gives it back to Alice. They put away their guns.

Jane and Xiao Liu sigh with relief as Alice
attaches the regulator to a tank and starts
to inflate a balloon.

The soldier's eyes are as wide as the
balloon.

Alice ties off five balloons, and they
float to the ceiling.
Ting, who's been on the upper berth hiding,
starts batting the balloons around the
compartment. The officers join in.

Everyone is all smiles.

                    XIAO LIU
          (in Chinese with English subtitles)
               So you see, no bomb, just
               hot air.

                    SOLDIER #2
               Nevertheless, you still need
               a permit for helium. I will
               have to confiscate these
               tanks.

Jane is translating in the background.
Alice is getting very agitated.

                    ALICE
               If my tanks leave this train,
               I'm going with them.

                    XIAO LIU
          Don't be foolish. Once they
          issue the permit, your tanks
          will be on the next train.

                     ALICE
          If they go, I go.

                                          CUT TO:

EXT. TRAIN STATION - CHINESE COUNTRYSIDE

Many students are clamoring to get on the
train as Alice, Ting, and Xiao Liu, with
all their belongings, try to get off.

Alice and Ting emerge from the crowd, but
Xiao Liu has been pushed back into the
train. She catches a glimpse of Fu Shan,
who has also been foiled in his attempt to
leave the train.

                     ALICE
                  (screaming)
          Xiao Liu!

A whistle blows, and the train starts to
leave. Students hang off the steps, blocking
the exit. A desperate Xiao Liu waves goodbye.

                    XIAO LIU
          See you in Beijing.

A panicked Alice turns to Ting.

                    ALICE
          What are we going to do?

                    TING
          Don't worry. We'll be fine.

Two local POLICE OFFICERS approach.

                POLICE OFFICER
      (in Chinese with English subtitles)
          You must come with us.

Ting translates. They pick up their bags
and follow the officers.

INT. GUILIN POLICE STATION - DAY

Alice, Ting, and the police officers enter.
A guard sits behind a counter and motions
for Alice to come forward.

Alice walks to the counter. It's so filthy
she can't put her purse down to sign the
papers that the guard hands her.

                    ALICE
          Ting, come here. I need
          you to tell me what these
          papers say.

                    TING
          (taking the papers from Alice)
          This is a permission form to
          test the tanks.

Alice signs the papers and hands them to
the guard.

                    ALICE
          Find out when we can get
          out of here. When's the next
          train?

                    TING
          Tomorrow.

                    ALICE
          Tomorrow?

                    TING
          Yes, there's only one train
          a day.

                    ALICE
          You mean we're stuck here. Do
          you have any money? I don't.

                    TING
          Me? I think I have something.

She reaches in her pocket and pulls out a
few coins to show Alice.

                    ALICE
          That's all? What are we going
          to do? Do you think they'll
          take my American Express
          Card?

Ting looks puzzled. Alice reaches into her
purse and pulls out her Gold Card.

                    ALICE
          Find out if we can use this
          card to pay for a hotel and
          food.

Ting takes the card and shows it to the
guards as she carries on an animated
conversation in Chinese with them. At first
she looks discouraged, then she lights up.

                    TING
          Don't worry. They will find a
          place for us to stay.

                                        CUT TO:

EXT. GUILIN COUNTRYSIDE - LI RIVER - DAY

Alice and Ting are in a small tour boat
with other Chinese tourists, and sampans
line the waterfront. It's very peaceful.
We see the ruins of a temple on the river
bank. They move slowly down the river,
casually trolling their fishing lines.

                    ALICE
I could think of worse places
to be stuck than this.

                    TING
You don't like Guilin? It's
the most beautiful place in
China.

                    ALICE
No, honey. It couldn't be more
perfect. I am feeling calmer
already.
                    (beat)
My kids and I never did
things like this.

                    TING
Don't people fish in America?

                    ALICE
Sure they do. I just never
had any time to play.
                    (beat)
My husband's right.

                    TING
About what?

                    ALICE
Working...where's it getting
me? Almost killed, that's
where.

Ting has something on her line. She's
excited.

Alice helps her reel in a 12" fish.

CLOSE ON FISH:

CUT TO:

EXT. HANCOCK PARK HOUSE - NIGHT

CLOSE ON FISH ON A BARBECUE:

Dave, clean shaven, with a new conservative
haircut and dress style, is flipping the
fish on the grill.

Todd, Julie, and Dawn are arguing as they
set the table.

                    TODD
          You gotta be kidding.

                    JULIE
          Oh, get off her case.

                    DAWN
          I know what I'm doing. I'm an
          artist.

                    TODD
          Yeh. Sure. Just like your dad.

                    DAVE
          This artist sold a large
          statue today. That's why
          you are having fresh salmon
          instead of canned.

                    TODD
          Even artists go to college.

                    DAWN
          It's none of your business.
          Already have one father
          nagging me.

Dave carries the fish on a platter as he
comes to the table.

                    DAVE
          Your brother's right. Listen
          to him.

                    DAWN
           Brother? He's not my brother.

                    DAVE
          If you want to be member of
          this family, get used to it.
          He's your brother.

He sits down and starts to debone the fish.

Julie comes up behind Dave and puts her
arms around his neck.

                    JULIE
          I'm all for that... Let's be a
          family.

Todd and Dawn glare at each other and at
Julie.

                                    CUT TO:

INT. APARTMENT LIVING ROOM - GUILIN - NIGHT

Alice, Ting, and three generations of
a CHINESE FAMILY crowd around a small
dinner table. It is a very small, sparsely
furnished room filled with little red clay
sculptures.

                    TING
          The grandfather told me this
          family's work is famous for
          hundreds of years in China.
          Their sculpture is in every
          museum.

                    ALICE
          Tell them my husband is also
          a sculptor and I know what a
          struggle it is for artists
          to earn a living.

                    TING
          Our new government gives
          artists money.

                    ALICE
        My husband would love that.

Ting and the family talk in Chinese.
The SON (10) selects a statue and shyly
hands it to Alice.

                    TING
            This boy is the youngest and
            wants you have his work as a
            gift.

Alice examines the sculpture and shows her
appreciation to the child with a great big
smile.

                    ALICE
            Ting, tell them that I am
            overwhelmed by their warm
            hospitality. We are total
            strangers, and they gave us a
            bed for the night, a wonderful
            meal, their friendship, and
            now this gift.

Ting translates, and the family nods and
smiles at Alice. Alice opens her purse
and pulls out several balloons. She blows
one up and hands it to the child. She
gives every family member a balloon, and
following her lead, they blow them up.

CUT TO:

EXT. GUILIN POLICE STATION - THE NEXT DAY

Alice and Ting are in a taxi as it
approaches the police station.

POV - ALICE

Hundreds of students crowd around the
entrance to the station. They are yelling
and holding their passports in the air.

The cab stops. Alice and Ting get out with
their bags as the cab drives away. They
walk over to a police officer who's trying
to control the crowd.

                    ALICE
                 (to Ting)
          Ask him where we pick up the
          tanks, and tell him we want
          a first-class compartment to
          Beijing.
                 (beat)
          And I need a bathroom.

Ting talks to the policeman as Alice looks
in amazement at the crowd. Some students
carry Peace signs and wear headbands. It's
a party atmosphere.

Ting looks discouraged from her
conversation with the police officer. She

motions to Alice that she's going through
the crowd to see what's happening. Alice
tries to stop her, but Ting is gone before
Alice can get to her.

The train approaches the station. Alice
looks nervously around for Ting. It's clear
that she really needs a toilet.

Alice reluctantly leaves her bags and
wades into the crowd, looking for a toilet.
Students surround her. They are Pushing to
get their travel documents, but they make
space for Alice to get through. She sees
Ting and calls out to her.

                    ALICE
          Ting, get us seats...here are
          the tickets!

Ting replies, but Alice cannot hear her
over the din of the crowd. A MALE STUDENT
next to Alice notices her dilemma.

                    STUDENT
          Give it to me. I'll get it
          to her.

Alice is relieved that someone speaks
English. She gives the student the tickets.

                    ALICE
          Is there a bathroom around
          here?

                    STUDENT
          Yes, by the train platform.

Alice is grateful and makes a quick exit
toward the train platform as the student
works his way through the crowd and gives
the tickets to Ting.
Alice has returned to the curb next to her
bags when Ting comes through the crowd
followed by three STUDENTS carrying Alice's
tanks.

Another STUDENT picks up the bags. She
pulls Alice by the arm, indication
that Alice should follow her. Alice is
reluctant.

                   STUDENT 2
          Come, we go Beijing now. OK?

Alice follows Ting and the entourage to the
train. They get on along with hundreds of
other students. The train pulls away in a
cloud of steam.

INT. TRAIN - DAY

POV - ALICE

Every seat is taken, and people sit on the
floor and in every corner. Children cry,
dogs bark, ducks in baskets quack... Alice
gets the picture. This isn't first class.

The students with Alice's bags and tanks
have found a place to sit. They motion for
Alice and Ting to join them. They squeeze
in beside the tanks. The seats are hard.
It's hot. It smells bad. Alice is not happy.

INT. TRAIN - NIGHT

Alice, Ting, and the students are asleep
when two PLA SOLDIERS wake them. Everyone's
papers are checked, but when they come to
Alice, they talk excitedly to one another
and gesture at her and her tanks. Alice
reaches into her purse for her papers
and gives them to the student who sits
facing her.

                    ALICE
          I've been through this before.
          Please show them these
          permits. Then they'll leave
          us alone.

The students gives the papers to the
soldiers. They look at them. They hand them
back to Alice and give her the once-over as
they leave.

                    STUDENT
          Why are you here? And what's
          in those tanks?

                    ALICE
I'm on a goodwill mission
bringing balloons to the
children's festival. That's
helium in those tanks.

                   STUDENT
Then we're all going to
Tiananmen Square.

                    ALICE
We are? Why are you going?

                   STUDENT
We're joining students from
all over China to pay tribute
to a great hero who has died.

                    ALICE
Oh, yes, I saw flags lowered
in his honor in Guangzhou.

                   STUDENT
And we're celebrating
democracy because that's what
he stood for.

                    ALICE
You all look like American
students in the '60s.

                   STUDENT
Yes. That was your peace
movement, wasn't it?

                    ALICE
          I marched. It was a very
          special time.

The student gets very excited as Alice
tells him of her involvement in the '60s.
He wakes his follow students.

                   STUDENT
          (in Chinese with English subtitles)
             Everyone! Wake up. We have an
             American peace demonstrator
             with us!

The other students wake up. They're all
excited as they gather around Alice and her
new friend.

Ting wakes up and joins the group.

                    ALICE
          I don't even know your name.
          I'm Alice Springer from
          California, USA.

                   STUDENT
          I'm Wen Chi Fu.

(turning to the other students one by one)

          And this is Zhang, this is
          Xiao, and this is Wai, Chu,
          Bing, and Lily —

Alice stops him in mid-sentence as she throws her hands up.

                    ALICE
          Wait a minute...wait a minute!
          I'll never remember all these
          names. Just tell me yours
          again...please!

                  WEN CHU FU
          I'm Wen Chu Fu, the leader of
          this group.

Many students open their bags and take out fruit, jelly jars, rice cakes, sweets, nuts, dried meats, fish, and thermos bottles.

Everybody shared, and Alice ends up holding a dried piece of fish. She doesn't want to eat it, but she also doesn't want to offend anyone...so she takes a bite and passes it to Ting. Ting eats the whole thing.

As they eat and share the food with Alice and Ting, the students are opening up. There is animated conversation between Wen Chu Fu and the students. By their gestures it's clear to Alice they're talking about her.

                  WEN CHU FU
          They have so many questions
          about your country and
          democracy.

                    ALICE
          What do they want to know?
          Where should I start?

                  WEN CHU FU
          Tell us about your Statue of
          Liberty...

                                        CUT TO:

EXT. MINISTER HAN'S COURTYARD - NIGHT

      CLOSE ON BALLOONS TIED TO CHAIRS:

Alice, Jane, Xiao Liu, Minister Han, and
MADAM HAN sit outside this centuries-old
hacienda-like home.

They are playing mah-jongg. Xiao Liu sits
behind Alice, coaching her.
Madam Han, in her 60s, has a smooth,
elegant, aristocratic bearing.

                    ALICE
          ...and Wen Chu Fu and his
          friends will probably be at
          the children's festival.

                  MADAM HAN
          How many students did
          you say...

Minister Han puts his hand over hers to quiet her.

She studies her hand then rearranges it as she puts in a tile from the wall.

                    MINISTER HAN
          We play a game of strategy in
          China.

                    ALICE
          Humm...nobody in China makes
          a move without thinking about
          the consequences...

She takes a tile from the wall, looks at it, and starts to put her rack.

                    ALICE
                 (continuing)
          I need to learn more about
          strategy.

                    XIAO LIU
          Keep the dragon and toss the
          crack.

He moves Alice's tiles, discards one, and forms a new sequence.

                    XIAO LIU
          Now this hand is worth more
          money.

                    ALICE
          Not mah-jongg! Business
          strategy.

                  MADAM HAN
          Are you here to do business?

                    JANE
          Yes, but MOFERT discouraged
          her. Takes too much money to
          build a new factory.

Jane throws a tile into the center, and
Madam Han picks it up and throws one of
her own.

                  MADAM HAN
          That's true. We only build
          new ones for matters of great
          importance...like the condom
          place we just built.

                    ALICE
          Condoms?!

The mah-jongg action has stopped.

                  MADAM HAN
          Yes, condoms are our primary
          form of birth control. We
          have a one-child rule because
          of our years of starvation.

                    ALICE
          Limiting population is good
          for the world.

They all nod in agreement.

Minister Han picks a tile from the wall,
rearranges his tiles, and lays them down.

                 MINISTER HAN
          Mah-jongg...

But no one reacts.

                  MADAM HAN
          Tso Tung, my aunt's boy, runs
          that factory. He's the head of
          our one-child commission.

Minister Han gets up from the table.

                    JANE
          Minister Tso! He's the one who
          told Alice no.

Madam Han looks at her husband as he walks
away from the table.

                  MADAM HAN
          He was always a good
          government worker, but...no
          imagination.

                    ALICE
               (enthusiastically)
          What if I used the old condom
          factory to make balloons?
          Invite him to the children's
          festival. He'll love the idea.

                  MADAM HAN
          I'll do my best. It will be no
          problem.

                  XIAO LIU
          Aha! You are learning Chinese
          strategy.

                    ALICE
          Yes, my strategy will make a
          lot of money.

Minister Han returns to the table.

                 MINISTER HAN
          Money? How about paying up.

They all look at him blankly.

                 MINISTER HAN
               (continuing)
          Mah-jongg... I won, remember?

They ante up.

The men excuse themselves and take the
maotai bottle. Alice, Madam Han, and Jane
continue their conversation.

EXT. COURTYARD - LATER THAT NIGHT

We see many glasses of tea on the table, the ash tray is filled with peanut shells, and the women are talking. Xiao Liu and Han enter the courtyard. Xiao Liu is tipsy, and Han has his arm around Xiao Liu's shoulder.

                    MINISTER HAN
          Students always march in the
          spring. Nothing will stop our
          gold deal.

He fills all the glasses.

                    MINISTER HAN
          One final toast before
          you go.

He raises his glass to the group.

                    MINISTER HAN
                    (continuing)
          To Dr. Barron and the gold
          deal. *Ganbei!*

The women all stand and drink. Xiao Liu leans on Alice for support.

CUT TO:

INT. BEIJING HOTEL - NIGHT

Alice has her arm around Xiao Liu to steady
him. His eyes are glazed.

                    ALICE
          Don't worry...*maotai* won't
          leave a hangover.

They stagger down the hall.

                    ALICE
                 (continuing)
          Now it's my turn to put you
          to bed.
                 (she laughs)

Xiao Liu stops and focuses his glazed eyes
on her. He straightens up, gaining control,
and pulls her as they continue down the
hall.

CUT TO:

EXT. TIANANMEN SQUARE - DAY

In an aerial view of this huge public
square (over 100 acres), we see Mao's tomb
and the monument to the People's Heroes, a
lofty granite statue.

To the west is the Great Hall of the
People. The Museum of History and the
Museum of the Chinese Revolution are to the
east. Behind the Gate of Heavenly Peace is
the Forbidden City, a huge maze of palaces
built in the 15th century.

The square is filled with thousands of
people. Tourist groups wait to enter
the Forbidden City, mothers wheel baby
carriages, fathers and sons fly kites,
vendors sell ice cream, and photographers
hawk their wares.

Alice and Jane stand at the middle of
the square and look toward Mao's tomb.
Thousands of students surround the People
Monument.

                    ALICE
          My friends from the train
          must be here.

                    JANE
          Maybe they already went home.
          I heard on the radio many
          students have left.

Alice sees Wen and his group in the center
of the crowd. She starts to move toward them.

                    ALICE
          There they are... There's Wen
          Chu Fu.

                    (beat)
          Hello, Wen. It's me, Alice...
          over here.

Wen notices Alice and motions for her to
join his group.
Alice pulls Jane along with her into the
group of students.

                    WEN
          What good fortune to see you
          at this moment!

He turns to the group.

                    WEN
                    (continuing)
          This is my American friend.
          She's seen the Statue of
          Liberty.

The students are excited as they talk to
each other and point at Alice. One of them
pulls a roll of paper out from under his
arm and unrolls it.

                    WEN
                    (to Alice)
          Come here. See what we are
          building.

Alice moves forward and looks at the
drawing. Jane follows her.

                    ALICE
          It's perfect likeness. How are
          you going to build it?

                    WEN
          We're looking for materials.
          Art students from the
          institute have promised to
          help.

                    ALICE
          I can get materials, but I
          also need the students help.
          Maybe we can work together.

                                      CUT TO:

MONTAGE:
An outside shot of the Art Institute.

Students with Alice making costumes.
Goddess of Democracy taking shape in the
back of the room.

Alice at the factory, getting her tanks
filled. Many ambulances line up, loading
tanks of oxygen.

More students pouring into Tiananmen
Square, a "Woodstock" atmosphere in
Beijing.

CUT TO:

EXT. TIANANMEN SQUARE - DAY

It's the children's festival. Schoolchildren
snake through the square, carrying their
balloons. The student demonstrators join in
the festivities.

Alice and her student helpers give helium-
filled friendship balloons to every
outstretched hand.

Fu Shan confronts Alice. He glares at her
and refuses to accept a balloon she offers.

Xiao Liu, Jane, Minister Han, Madam Han,
and Minister Tso, Madam Han's cousin, are
in the reviewing stand.

Ting and the children do the dragon dance.
They weave in and out of all the people,
carrying a green balloon dragon head.

Minister and Madam Han smile and applaud
at Ting's dancing. Minister Tso is also
enjoying the show. He turns to Madam Han.

                    MINISTER TSO
          These balloons are wonderful.

                    MADAM HAN
          She'd like to visit your old
          condom factory tomorrow. Let

her. It might do you some
good.

Alice joins the family in the reviewing
stand.

                    ALICE
          The college kids added so
          much to the excitement.
                    (beat)
          Are they in danger? I've seen
          soldiers, ambulances, and
          oxygen tanks.

The subject is ignored. Nobody responds.

                    JANE
                    (after a beat)
          Minister Tso wants to
          manufacture balloons.
          Tomorrow you can visit his
          factory.

                    ALICE
                    (poking Xiao Liu)
          Did you hear? Everything's
          turning out perfectly.

                    XIAO LIU
          See, patience pays.
                    (He mumbles an aside)
          Turning condoms into
          balloons. Very clever
          Americans.

Alice squeezes Xiao Liu's hand.

Just then, many balloons are released to fly over the city. The children grab adults to dance with them including some Chinese soldiers. One of them pulls away.

Xiao Liu sees Fu Shan and looks concerned.

Fu Shan looks right at them. He takes out his book and writes into it.

                    ALICE
                 (pointing)
        Fu Shan's following me. What's
        this all about?

                  Xiao Liu
                (whispering)
        Shh...not here. Later. We'll
        talk later.

Xiao Liu leans over to speak to Minister Han.

He turns back to Alice.

                  XIAO LIU
                (continuing)
        The Chinese say you haven't
        visited China if you don't
        see the Great Wall.

EXT. GREAT WALL - JIN SHAN LING - DAY

Alice and Xiao Liu are alone on a ridge
overlooking a deep beautiful valley.

                    ALICE
          Oh, this is spectacular!

He moves closer to her and takes her hand.

                    ALICE
              (pulling away)
          You dragged me all the way
          out here to tell me why Fu
          Shan is following us?

                  XIAO LIU
          Ears are everywhere but not
          in this wall.

                    ALICE
          All right! So what were
          you two fighting about in
          Guangzhou?

                  XIAO LIU
          The gold deal. Fu Shan is
          against it.

                    ALICE
          I saw him on the train. What
          does he want with me?

                    XIAO LIU
He wanted to stop you from
getting to Beijing and
Minister Han.

                     ALICE
Why? What did I do?

                    XIAO LIU
It's political. Their whole
group is against China doing
business with the West.

                     ALICE
I thought China wanted
America money.

                    XIAO LIU
With all the changes going
on in Beijing, it's hard to
know what they want. And you
better stop your involvement
with the students. It's
dangerous.

                     ALICE
But I believe in what in what
they're doing.

He takes her hand and stares up the wall.

                    XIAO LIU
                  (continuing)
        Come on, listen to me. I
        don't want anything to happen
        to you.

He pulls her toward him. He kisses her
gently on the mouth. She responds.

INT. BEIJING HOTEL- NIGHT

Alice and Xiao Liu are outside her room,
arm in arm. She's wearing a T-shirt saying,
"I walked the Great Wall of China."

She opens her door to see the room has
been RANSACKED. She screams, and Xiao Liu
pushes her inside.

                    ALICE
                  (screaming)
        My things, my things! Look at
        this room.

Xiao Liu puts his hand over her mouth and
turns on the radio then pulls her toward
the bathroom. He points to the smoke
detector.

                    XIAO LIU
                  (whispering)
        Quiet. Stop screaming.

INT. BEIJING HOTEL ALICE'S
BATHROOM - EVENING

Xiao Liu turns on the shower and sits Alice
down on the closed toilet and takes his
hand away from her mouth.

> XIAO LIU
> We don't want public security
> involved until we know what's
> going on.

> ALICE
> (whispers)
> What's going on?

> XIAO LIU
> They're looking to see if
> you're a spy.

Xiao Liu sits down on the edge of the tub.

> ALICE
> Who's looking?

> XIAO LIU
> It could be Fu Shan's people
> trying to link you with the
> pro-democracy movement.

> ALICE
> But why?

                    XIAO LIU
          He will do anything he can
          to discredit you and have you
          thrown out of China.

                    ALICE
          What are we going to do?

                    XIAO LIU
          I'll talk to Minister Han. His
          forces can take care of Fu
          Shan and Chen.

Xiao Liu turns off the water. They walk out
of the bathroom to the door.

                    ALICE
          I'm really scared. Don't
          leave me.

                    XIAO LIU
          They've already been here.
          They won't return tonight.

                    ALICE
          But you will, won't you.

She gives him a longing glance. He kisses
her and leaves. Alice closes the door,
locks it, and turns to survey the damage.

INT. BEIJING HOTEL LOBBY - DAY

Alice is dressed for business as she gets
off the elevator. She sees Fu Shan at the
information counter talking to the CLERK.
She hides behind a pillar until he heads
for the elevator. She approaches the clerk.

                    ALICE
          Is there a message for Alice
          Springer, room 1408?

                    CLERK
          Yes, a man just asked for you.

                    ALICE
          No, a message from Mr. Ping...
          Xiao Liu Ping, room 1540.

He checks the files and comes back very
quickly.

                    CLERK
          No, no message, Miss Springer.
          Mr. Ping has check out.

We see a man enter the lobby carrying a
sign "Alice Springer."

                    ALICE
          Oh, no. That can't be.

                    CLERK
Sorry, miss, last night he
check out.

                    ALICE
              (with urgency)
I must speak to Minister Han.
Can you get him on the phone?

                    CLERK
Who?

                    ALICE
Minister Han Xue Wen. He's
a very important man in
Beijing.

                    CLERK
What ministry he head?

                    ALICE
              (frazzled)
I think it's called Ministry
of Foreign Trade for mining
and metals.

                    CLERK
You have his phone number?

                    ALICE
No, but his house is quite
close to here.

                    CLERK
          Sorry, madam...without number
          can't help you.

Alice is tapped on the shoulder. Startled,
she turns around to see a UNIFORMED MAN.

                    ALICE
          Oh! Do you have a message
          from Xiao Liu for me?

                    CLERK
          Madam, this is driver. You
          Miss Springer? He come to
          take you somewhere.

He speaks in Chinese to the driver. The
driver responds.

                    CLERK
                 (continues)
          You visit condom factory?

                    ALICE
                 (embarrassed)
          Yes, but I must leave a
          message for Mr. Ping. Will you
          please see that he gets it?

                    CLERK
          I tell you he check out last
          night, but I hold message if
          you insist.

Alice writes a note, gives it to the clerk, and leaves with the driver.

                                      CUT TO:

EXT. CONDOM FACTORY - DAY

We see a five-story cement building with billowing smoke stacks and trucks parked in front of a guarded, gated entrance.

The GUARD stops the car, and the driver gets out. Much conversation takes place while Alice anxiously waits in the back seat.

Finally, they return to the car.

The guard bows slightly to Alice and gives directions in Chinese to the driver, who gets in the car.

The gate opens and the car goes up the road to the administration office.

INT. CONDOM FACTORY - DAY

It looks like a candy factory. Shower-capped women in white coats dip cylindrical objects into vats of liquid rubber.

Alice, Minister Tso, FOUR CHINESE MEN, and
one WOMAN are watching the condoms come
off the conveyor belt.

A man explains the process to Alice and
Minister Tso.
The woman is translating.

As Alice takes a condom off the belt, she
smiles, pulls it open, and stretches it
out, inspecting it carefully.

                    ALICE
          I'd like to bring some samples
          to my American manufacturer.

The woman translates.

                    MINISTER TSO
          Of course, and I'd like to
          discuss a letter of intent
          with you now.

The woman talks to the workers as she
pulls several packages of condoms off the
assembly line. She gives them to Alice.

INT. BALLOON FANTASIES OFFICE- LOS
ANGELES - DAY

Susan is pulling a box of balloons off the
shelf as Dave and Dawn watch. She hands
the box to Dave. Dawn grabs a balloon out
of the box and blows it up.

                    DAWN
          Oh, Dad, look...it's just like
          I designed them.

As she blows up the balloon, it becomes a
panda head.

                    DAVE
          A chip off the old block.

                    SUSAN
          What do you know? This kid's
          really got talent.

                    DAVE
          These will be perfect for
          the zoo.

                    SUSAN
          The zoo? Alice is going to
          sell a billion of these in
          China.

                    DAVE
          First things first. How much
          are they, and how soon can we
          get them?

                    DAWN
          Don't forget my cut.

                    DAVE
          Not...another businesswoman in
          the family!

                                   CUT TO:

INT. BEIJING CONDOM FACTORY MEETING
ROOM - DAY

Alice, Minister Tso, and the woman are at
a conference table. The woman gathers up
some papers. Alice puts other papers in her
briefcase.

                 MINISTER TSO
          The letter of intent in
          English will be delivered to
          your hotel tomorrow.

The meeting is over. They are all smiles
as they talk among themselves with great
animation.

                    ALICE
          Thank you so much. I can't
          tell how happy I am.

The woman brings in some *maotai* and
glasses. She pours a glass for all present.
They all toast to the new venture.

                    ALICE
          Could you send a message to
          my office?

                    WOMAN
          Yes, our FAX is available
          to you.

                    ALICE
                 (dictates)
          Condom Factory approves
          letter of intent to
          manufacture our balloons.
          Everything great. Love.
          Alice.

The woman nods in understanding.

                    ALICE
          Thank you. Now you're sure it
          will go out today?

EXT. CONDOM FACTORY - DAY

The workers from the factory wave goodbye holding balloons as Alice's limo goes through the gate. We see Fu Shan drive up and stop at the gate after her car leaves.

CUT TO:

INT. ALICE'S LIMO - DAY

On the way back to the Beijing Hotel, they turn the corner into Changan Avenue. Alice can see the hotel in the distance, but thousands of people block the street.

                    DRIVER
          No go, missy.

Alice tries to get out of the car, but the door is locked.

                    DRIVER
          We go Han house.

CUT TO:

INT. HAN HOUSE - NIGHT

Minister Han, Madam Han, and Alice watch the news on television. Alice is wearing Madam Han's kimono.

CLOSE ON TV:

Millions of people parade toward Tiananmen Square. They carry banners and signs as they pass the Beijing Hotel.

>   ALICE
> Will I be able to get to the
> hotel tomorrow?

>   MINISTER HAN
> Tomorrow is the day we visit
> our ancestors' graves. The
> streets will be even more
> crowded.

>   ALICE
> But my letter of intent
> should be there.

>   MINISTER HAN
> Not likely. All factories will
> be closed.

                    ALICE
          ...and, I have to see if Xiao
          Liu left me a message.

                    MINISTER HAN
          We're all waiting to hear
          from him. He probably couldn't
          get through the streets last
          night, and there's no way now.
                    (beat)
          Join us, then we'll get you
          back to the hotel.

                                        CUT TO:

EXT. CEMETERY - DAY

It's a centuries-old place with shrines,
overgrown headstones, pagodas, and rocky
garden paths set in a valley in the
countryside outside of Beijing.

Family groups are gathered around graves
as flowers, fruits, and incense are offered
in traditional remembrance. The women are
sweeping off the graves while the men and
children picnic nearby.

Madam Han, Alice, and the driver are
gathering the remains of their picnic in
preparation for leaving. Minister Han lies
on the grass, napping.

                    MADAM HAN
                    (to Alice)
          Have you seen Ting? We need
          to leave.

                     ALICE
          I saw her playing on the
          hill. I'll get her.

Alice leaves and starts up the hill.

At the top of the hill, Alice stops to look
around. She sees a great cloud of dust
in the distance. She continues to look,
and the dust reveals tanks followed by
thousands of marching soldiers. Alice is
mesmerized by what she sees.

Ting comes up behind Alice and grabs on to
her. Alice is startled.

                     ALICE
          Oh! It's you. You scared me.

                     TING
          Why? I'm not a ghost.

Alice sweeps her up in her arms, turns,
and runs down the hill.

                     ALICE
          Well, I'm spooked, and it's
          time to go home.

CUT TO:

INT. MINISTER HAN HOUSE - NIGHT

The adults are sitting around the kitchen
table by the telephone. Alice is dialing.
She waits then holds the receiver out so
all can hear the busy signal.

                    ALICE
          Do you think I'll ever get
          through? Maybe I'll have
          better luck at the hotel.

                    MINISTER HAN
          Try one more time.
               (he looks at his watch)
          Your plane's not leaving for
          four hours.

                    ALICE
               (as she dials again)
          But I'm worried about you...
          the army...Oh! Oh! It's
          ringing.

She pulls a paper from Han's hand and
nervously scans it.

                    ALICE
               (yelling)
          Dave... It's me. Can you
          hear me?
                    (beat)

Yes...I'm fine...don't worry.
            (beat)
Tonight, I'll be on flight
number
      (she looks at the paper)
0020 United landing at...
            (beat)
Dave are you there?

She flicks the receiver up and down.

                ALICE
      Hello, hello?
                (turns to Han)
      there's only static on the
      line.

                MINISTER HAN
      Come on, you've got to get
      out of here. Things are
      getting grim.

                                    CUT TO:

INT. BEIJING HOTEL - ALICE'S ROOM - NIGHT

Alice's open suitcases are on the bed. Her
clothes, her purse, and the box of condoms
are in a pile next to them.

As she frantically stuffs her things into
the case, she breaks her nail. She stops,
winces, and looks at her hand.

                         ALICE
          Oh! Damn.

She finds her toilet kit under the pile,
rummages into it, and pulls out a tube of
nail glue. She starts to repair the nail.

There's a knock at the door. Alice goes
to answer. She sees the back of a Chinese
student running down the hall. She notices
an envelope he has left on the floor.

She picks it up and closes the door.

She opens the envelope, takes out a note,
and a microdot falls out.

                    CLOSE ON NOTE:

"Alice this microdot contains the names of
the student democracy leaders, sympathetic
government officials and our military
supporters. These people are the future of
our movement and must not be purged by the
government. Please guard this with your
life and take it to Los Angeles with you.
My colleague in Los Angeles will contact
you. They will find you. We will never give
up, we will be free." Wen Chu Fu

A POUNDING on the door startles her.

                    VOICE (O.S.)
          Open the door, public
          security! Open up!

Alice picks up the microdot, her purse,
the glue, the condoms, and runs into the
bathroom.

INT. BATHROOM, ALICE'S ROOM, BEIJING
HOTEL - NIGHT

She locks the door and turns on the shower.

She rips up the note and flushes it down
the toilet.
She takes a condom package and opens it
carefully with her nail file.

The POUNDING is louder.

She places the microdot inside the tip of
a condom, closes the package, and glues
it shut with her nail glue then puts the
condom package back into the box.

As Alice puts the condom box into her
purse, she hears the door to her room
give way.

She removes her robe and jumps into the
shower.

The POUNDING continues at the bathroom door.

A woman's VOICE is HEARD above the water.

                    VOICE (O.S.)
          Open this door immediately!
          Public security.

Alice grabs a towel, gets out of the
shower, and opens the door a crack.

POV - ALICE

There are three official-looking MEN and
one WOMAN standing by the door.

                    ALICE
          What do you want? I was in
          the shower.

                    WOMAN
          Get dressed. You're coming
          with us.

                    ALICE
          I'll need some clothes to
          wear.

The three men speak to each other in
Chinese as they search through her
belongings. As each garment is cleared, one
of the men puts it in Alice's suitcase.

                    ALICE
                 (thinking)
           Why are they going through my
           things?

The woman picks up a dress and hands it to
Alice through the bathroom door.

                    WOMAN
           Take this dress and put it
           on. No more questions.

INT. ALICE'S ROOM - BEIJING HOTEL - NIGHT

The public security officers continue
their search as the woman finishes packing
Alice's belongings.

The bathroom door opens. Alice enters the
room, purse in hand.

                    ALICE
           Why are you here? I must make
           a phone call.

                    WOMAN
           No questions. Come now, Miss
           Springer.

Alice reluctantly leaves the room escorted
by the woman and followed by the three men
who carry her suitcase.

INT. PUBLIC SECURITY BUILDING INTERROGATIONS
ROOM - NIGHT

Alice sits at a table in the center of the
room. The contents of her purse are spread
about. The box of condoms is in full view.

One uniformed OFFICIAL sits at the
table with Alice. Several other MEN in
shirtsleeves and sandals stand in the
background, observing and writing notes
into a book.

> OFFICIAL
> You've been seen with the
> students who are causing the
> trouble. And we have learned
> that your room was broken
> into.

> ALICE
> Is that why I've been
> arrested? I'm not a criminal.
> I'm a guest in your country.

> OFFICIAL
> Quiet! We ask the questions!

He reaches into his jacket pocket and
brings out a stack of photos.

                    OFFICIAL
          Now we will talk about your
          association with one Wen
          Chu Fu.

He spreads the photos on the table. They're
pictures of Alice and Wen all over Beijing
and even one from the train.

Alice is visibly shaken.

SOUNDS of gunfire and armored vehicles
suddenly fill the room. Everyone is
startled. The official turns to his
observers.

                    OFFICIAL
          (in Chinese with English subtitles)
            What's going on! Find out!

Three of the observers run out of the
room, leaving the door open.
Alice stuffs her things back into her
purse.

The SOUNDS get louder. People outside the
room scream in terror.
Another OFFICIAL runs in the room and
excitedly confronts the interrogator.

                    OFFICIAL 2
          (in Chinese with English subtitles)
            Put her in a safe place! We
            must protect her.

                              ALICE
                What's going on? Somebody tell
                me what's happening!

The two officials grab Alice and pull her
out of the room.

Alice is kicking and screaming as she goes,
purse in hand.

INT. PUBLIC SECURITY - SOLITARY CONFINEMENT
CELL - NIGHT

Alice sits on her bed in a small square
sparse solitary cell. A single bulb lights
the room.

Alice HEARS GUNFIRE off-screen. It's getting
louder and louder — first faintly then
louder. The SOUND of thousands of POUNDING
FEET sweep by her cell.

People scream off-screen as guns pop.

Alice grabs the cell bars and shakes them.

                              ALICE
                Let me out! I'm just a
                businesswoman from America.
                I'm not a spy! Please
                              (beat)
                someone listen.

Alice trembles, wraps herself in a blanket, and backs into the corner.

                    ALICE
                 (to herself)
          All I wanted was to save my
          house, and now I may never
          see my family again.

                                        CUT TO:

INT. LAX - INTERNATIONAL ARRIVAL
TERMINAL - DAY

Dave, Dawn, Julie, and Todd wait for
Alice's arrival. Dawn is transformed into
a neat teenager. She's wearing a tee-shirt
with the logo "Alice's Wonderland."

They watch as the last of the passengers
come through customs. No Alice.

Dave stops the last PASSENGER. The kids
gather round.

                    DAVE
          Is there anyone left in
          customs from Beijing?

                    PASSENGER
          No, I was the last one
          through.

                    JULIE
          Didn't you see my mom? She
          was supposed to be on this
          flight!

Julie's getting agitated and turns to Dave.
Her look says, "Do something!"

                    TODD
          Let's check the passenger
          manifesto.

                    DAWN
          Manifest, dummy!

                    DAVE
          Let's ask the ticket agent.

They all walk over to the United Airlines
counter.

                    DAVE
          What's happening in Beijing?
          My wife was to be on that
          flight.

                    CLERK
          I'm sorry, sir, I'm not
          authorized to give out any
          information.

                    DAVE
          That's ridiculous! Did she
          board that plane?

Julie steps up to the counter with a big
smile on her face.

                    JULIE
          Why can't you tell us where
          my mom is?

Dave, Dawn, Todd, and Julie talk and once.

                    DAVE
          Was her name on the list?

                    TODD
          Did she get sick on the
          plane?

                    DAWN
          Did someone Kidnap her in
          Japan?

                    CLERK
          Hold it! She never boarded
          in Beijing, and all our phone
          lines to China are down. I'm
          sorry...that's all I know.

The clerk turns to leave.

Julie starts to cry, and Todd throws a
tantrum.

                    TODD
          Don't you turn your back on
          me. It's my mother...

Dave puts his arm around Julie and the other hand on Todd's shoulder.

             DAVE
       Come on, kids, this won't
       help. We'll find Mom...even if
       I have to call the president
       of the United States.

                                    CUT TO:

INT. PUBLIC SECURITY BUILDING FOYER - THE NEXT DAY

Jane and Alice are with the interrogating official who now sits behind a desk, looking very weary and disheveled. Their conversation is in Chinese (with English subtitles).

             JANE
       Well, she Finally convinced
       you to let her go.

             OFFICIAL
       But she has not answered our
       question.

             ALICE
             (in English)
       And she will not.

                    JANE
          She must be released now. I
          act under Minister Han Xue
          Wen's authority.

She presents the official with document. He
takes it, glances at it, and nods his head
in the affirmative.

                  OFFICIAL
          You may take her, but she
          must leave the country
          immediately!

Alice and Jane leave. Fu Shan appears from
behind a screen and confronts the official.

                  FU SHAN
      (in Chinese with English subtitles)
          I understand you have no
          choice but to let her go.
          Don't worry. If she has the
          list, I will get it.

                  OFFICIAL
          But she's going to America.

                  FU SHAN
          And I will follow her. All
          she cares about is money.
          It will be easy to get the
          information from her.

INT. MINISTER HAN'S LIMO - DAY

Jane, Alice, Ting, Minister and Madam Han
sit in the back.

                    MINISTER HAN
          I've arranged for you to leave
          immediately for Los Angeles.

                    JANE
          The wind has blown clouds
          over the sun, and you are
          no longer safe here. Look
          outside...

POV - ALICE

We see tanks moving into positions at
intersections guarded by armed soldiers. As
the car moves slowly toward the airport,
more troops come into view. There are no
pedestrians or bicycles, only soldiers.

                    ALICE
          I heard guns and screams last
          night. Is there a war?

                    MINISTER HAN
          Our government called it a
          disturbance by hooligans.
          I say it's the old men
          protecting their power.

Madam Han motions toward the driver and
puts her finger to her lips.

                    MADAM HAN
                  (whispering)
          Careful, the seeds of fear
          may fall into fertile ground.

                    JANE
          Your husband has many
          powerful friends. Don't worry.

                    MINISTER HAN
          In my life, I have seen many
          things. Change in my beloved
          China is like the tortoise.
          It moves very slowly but lives
          forever.

Alice looks at Han.

                    ALICE
          Where's Xiao Liu? I fear for
          his safety.

                    MINISTER HAN
          He's safely out of the
          country.

As the limo stops in front of the airport
departure gate, Alice hugs Ting with great
sadness.

CUT TO:

EXT. DEPARTURE TERMINAL BEIJING
AIRPORT - DAY

Chaos is everywhere. Horns honk, people
yell, baggage is piled all over the
sidewalk, blocking the entrance.

Jane, Alice, and the driver make their way
through the crowd, carrying bags. The driver
clears a path, and they enter the terminal

INT. BEIJING AIRPORT GATE - DAY

Jane and Alice hug and tearfully say
goodbye.
Alice shows the ticket to the attendant and
waves a final goodbye.
The terminal is empty. Alice is on the
plane when we see Fu Shan. He is the last
person to board.

INT. LAX INTERNATIONAL TERMINAL ARRIVAL
AREA - DAY

A long line of Chinese people come through
the doors at immigration followed by
Alice. They are immediately surrounded
by REPORTERS and minicams. She is tired
disheveled and confused by all the
attention.

                    REPORTER #1
Miss, miss, what's going on in
China?

                    REPORTER #2
How did you get out of
Beijing?

                    REPORTER #3
Are you the only American on
this plane?

                      ALICE
Please, please, I just want to
get home. Leave me alone.

Fu Shan moves in on Alice, sees the
reporters, and makes a fast retreat. Alice
does not notice.

                    REPORTER #2
We heard the airport was
sealed to foreigners.

Alice fights her way out through the crowd.

Reporter #2 follows.

                    REPORTER #2
How did you get on the plane?

Alice hands him her bags.

                    ALICE
          Get me home and I'll tell you
          my story.

                                      CUT TO:

INT ALICE'S BEDROOM - THE NEXT MORNING

Alice sits on her bed, surrounded by the
family.

                    DAWN
          ...and then what happened?

                    ALICE
          They threw me in a cell,
          locked the door, and left me.

                    TODD
          Those Chinese bastards.

                    ALICE
          They were just doing their
          job. It's the hardliners
          calling the shots.

                    JULIE
          Tiananmen Square looked like
          a "Dead" concert parking lot
          to me.

                    DAVE
          It looked more like Woodstock
          to me.

                    ALICE
        I can't get used to you
        without your beard.

She runs her hand over his chin then pulls
him closer to her.

                    DAVE
        You'll get used to the new me.

                    ALICE
        You should have come with me
        to China. I missed you.

Tears start to well up in her eyes as she
pulls Dave closer to her.

                    ALICE
        Those kids were just like we
        were in the '60s
                    (beat)
        and just like you kids and
        your friends are now...

She reaches out and draws her children closer.
The phone rings. Dave answers it.

He listens then covers the mouthpiece with
his hand.

                    DAVE
        It's Dr. Barron. He read your
        story in this morning's paper.
        Do you want to talk to him?

Alice takes the phone.

                    ALICE
          Uh-huh, yes.
                    (she listens)
          Oh really? Thank you.
                    (beat)
          Tomorrow morning at 10:00 will
          be fine. I'll see you then.

She hangs up the phone.

                    DAVE
          What did he want?

                    ALICE
          My letter came from China.
          They want to go forward with
          the deal.

                    DAVE
          Honey, that's wonderful!

Alice gets up and starts to pace around.

                    ALICE
          Well, I'm having second
          thoughts.

Todd angrily confronts her.

                    TODD
You're not gonna do it? I
thought we're broke. You have
to go for it.

                    ALICE
I don't have to do anything.
If there's one thing I
learned in China, it's that
there's more to life than
money.

                    JULIE
Whatever you decide, Mom, I'm
with you.

                    DAVE
I don't understand. You worked
so hard to get this deal.
You're just jetlagged.

                    ALICE
It was important before, but
now everything's changed.
Family and tradition come
first.

Alice sits down determinedly.

                    TODD
Great, how are we going to
survive on that?

                    DAWN
          Your mom's business is better
          than you think. If we all
          work together as a family,
          we'll be fine.

                    ALICE
          I've got to figure out how to
          handle tomorrows' meeting.
          I'll see you all later.

                                        CUT TO:

INT. BARRON'S OFFICE - DAY

Alice, Xiao Lu, and Barron are each reading
a copy of her letter of intent from the
condom factory.

                    BARRON
          It will take at least another
          two years before final
          approval from the central
          government.

                    ALICE
          That's OK. I don't want the
          deal.

                    BARRON
          That's how the Chinese do
          business.

                    ALICE
Didn't you hear what I just
said? I don't even want to do
business there. A government
that hurts its people isn't
going to make money off me.

                    XIAO LIU
You did a remarkable job.
Take this contract. You've
earned it.

                    ALICE
No, I won't. I can't work with
those...barbarians.

                    BARRON
Alice, don't be a fool. In two
years, it will be business as
usual. No one will remember.

                    ALICE
No, it's not for me, but thank
you for the opportunity. I
learned so much. I'll be
grateful.

EXT. BARRON INDUSTRIES ENTRANCE - DAY

Xiao Liu and Alice exit the building and
stand in front on stairs.

ALICE

Are you so callous and
insensitive that you want me
to take this deal?

XIAO LIU

Come on, Alice, this is
business. I thought you
needed the money.

ALICE

I don't understand. You've
experienced oppressive
repression, yet now you
support it.

XIAO LIU

I'm like a piece of silk.
I flow with the winds. It's
the only way I know how to
survive.

ALICE

Goodbye, Xiao Liu. *Zaijian*
(goodbye). *Xiexie* (thank you).

The valet is there with her car.

CUT TO:

INT. ALICE'S HOUSE - KITCHEN - DAY :

Dave is at the table, making a fruit punch in a large bowl. Alice is getting cups to bring outside. Many of Todd's and Julie's friends are outside around the pool at a graduation party.

Off-screen, we hear a DOORBELL RING.

                    ALICE
        (yelling out the kitchen door)
        Todd, someone's at the door.

She puts the finishing on a platter of food and brings it outside. Dave follows, carrying the punch bowl.

EXT. ALICE'S BACKYARD - DAY

Todd's and Julie's friends, 30 to 40 CALIFORNIA KIDS, are playing volleyball and swimming. Einstein runs around the pool and barks at the swimmers. Fu Shan, disguised as a Chinese student with long hair, sunglasses, and a headband, stands on the patio, taking in the scene.

                    TODD
        This guy's here to see you.

Fu Shan greets Alice.

                    ALICE
          Hello, I've been expecting a
          friend of Wen Chu Fu.

                    DAVE
          Didn't I see you on TV in
          Beijing? Weren't you one of
          the leaders?

                    FU SHAN
          You might have seen me. I was
          there with some other UCLA
          students.

                    ALICE
          You must want the list.

Dave pulls out a chair..

                    DAVE
          Here, sit down please.

                    ALICE
          I'll be right back.

Alice leaves. Fu Shan sits down.

                    DAVE
          Can I get you something
          to eat?

                    FU SHAN
        I'd like tea, if you have
        some.

                    DAVE
        No problem.

Dave goes to the kitchen. Three GUESTS join
Fu Shan on the patio.

                    FU SHAN
        Great party!

                    GIRL #1
        I heard you were in Beijing.
        How exciting!

                    GIRL #2
        How did you get out? We've
        heard they closed the borders.

                    FU SHAN
        I have a student visa. I'm a
        Bruin like you.

                    GUY #1
        Hey, dude! Out of sight!

He gives him a high five.

                    GUY #1
                  (continues)
        Where were you when the tanks
        started to roll?

                        FU SHAN
                 Defending the Goddess of
                 Democracy.

Alice approaches the patio, takes in the
scene, and is happy to see Fu Shan enjoying
himself.

                        ALICE
                 Honey, would you get Todd
                 for me?

                        GIRL #1
                 Sure, Mrs. Springer.
                        (beat)
                      (to Fu Shan)
                 Come on with me. I want to
                 introduce you to my friends.

They leave as Dave returns with the tea.

                        DAVE
                 I made him the tea. I bet
                 what he really wanted was
                 beer.

Alice has the open box of condoms in her
hand. She looks upset as Todd come to the
patio.

                        TODD
                 So, what do you want?

                    ALICE
          They're gone. Three packages
          are missing. They were here
          last night.

                    TODD
          So what? You've got a gross.

                    ALICE
          I hid the microdot in a
          condom, and now it's gone.

                    TODD
          Easy come, easy go.

                    ALICE
          Very funny.

She gives him a wry, bemused look. Todd
reaches in his pocket.

                    TODD
          Here, I still have one.

He hands her a condom package. Alice looks
at it.
                    ALICE
          That's not the one.

                    TODD
          Candy and Bob went upstairs.
          I hope I get there in time.

                    ALICE
     You better.

She gives him a shove, and he runs into the
house. She heads for Fu Shan by the pool.
He is surrounded by bikini-clad girls.

                    ALICE
          Todd's looking for the list.
          It'll be a few minutes.

                    FU SHAN
          It's OK. I'm having a great
          time.

                    GIRL #1
          Oh, Mrs. Springer, we're so
          glad you brought him.

                    GIRL #2
          He's a hero.

                    GIRL #3
          It's was so dangerous for him.

She gives each of the GIRLS the once-
over. The one on his lap runs her fingers
through his hair.

                    ALICE
          I see you've adjusted to
          Western ways. How long did
          say you've been in this
          country?

The student nervously pushes the girl off his lap. His sunglasses fall off, revealing the face of Fu Shan!

                    ALICE
          Oh my god! It's you!

                    GIRL #1
          What's going on?

Fu Shan pulls off his wig and pulls out a gun.

                    GIRL #3
          Ehhhhh!
                    (screams)

Dave runs over.

                    ALICE
          Stand back! He has a gun.

                    GIRL #3
          Ehhhhh!
                    (screams again)

Einstein charges Fu Shan and knocks him into the pool. He drops his gun as he falls. Alice picks it up.

                    DAVE
          Hey, you guys, grab him!

                    SWIMMER #1
          What's going on?

                      ALICE
          He's with Chinese secret
          police.

                    SWIMMER #2
          I'll get the bastard.

The SWIMMERS drag Fu Shan out of the pool.
Dave pushes Fu Shan against the wall and
searches him then shoves him into a chair.

A triumphant Todd runs out on the patio,
holding an unrolled condom.

                      TODD
          I got it!
                    (beat)
          What's going on?

                    GIRL #1
          This hero is a spy.

                      DAVE
          He followed your mother from
          Beijing.

Todd grabs Fu Shan out of the chair and
pushes him into the pool house. Everyone
follows. The GUESTS inside watching
television are surprised.

                    TODD
         While your generation is
         fighting for democracy, you
         support the hardliners.

                    FU SHAN
         I know Western democracy will
         corrupt China.

                    ALICE
                    (beat)
         Todd! let him alone.
                    (to Fu Shan)
         My family's sympathy is with
         your people. Violence solves
         nothing.

Todd releases Fu Shan.

Fu Shan straightens his clothes.

                    FU SHAN
         Money solves everything with
         you people. How much do you
         want for the list?

                    ALICE
         You seemed to think I'm easy
         to corrupt. Think again.

The television has caught Alice's attention.
Peter Jennings is doing a recap of
Tiananmen Square.

                    ALICE
            Turn up the sound.

Fu Shan notices the television.

Todd and his friends talk at once.

                    TODD
            See what freedom means...

                    GIRL #1
            Ability to have a big
            family...

                BEACH GIRL #2
            Choosing a career...

                    BOY #1
            Living wherever you want...

                    TODD
            Your people are dying
            for it....

                  FU SHAN
            These are just tricks of your
            Western media.

Suddenly Fu Shan stops and looks intently
at the screen. There is pandemonium as
tanks roll into the square then a close up
of a girl crying.

                    FU SHAN
          That's my sister. What have
          they done to her?

Peter Jennings return to the screen. A
defeated Fu Shan slumps down on the couch.

                                CUT TO:

INT. KITCHEN - TWO DAYS LATER - DAY

Dave is at the stove, making omelet. The
rest of the family is gathered around the
table.

                    DAVE
          What's going to happen to Fu
          Shan?

                    ALICE
          He can't go back to China.
          He's lost face. Wen's friend
          finally has the list.

                    DAWN
          My mother's Zen master told
          me: if something falls down a
          well, the only way to retrieve
          it is to fall in after it.

Todd gives her a "there she goes again"
look.

                    TODD
          He's already been in the
          pool, and if you had a face
          like that, wouldn't you want
          to lose it?

Dave brings the platter with the omelet to
the table. Todd sticks his fork in to taste
it. Julie gives him a look of disproval.

                    JULIE
          Poor Fu Shan. Where will
          he go?

                    ALICE
          He'll probably ask for
          political asylum.

Dave serves the omelet to everybody•

                    DAVE
          Yeh, and he'll open a
          restaurant and move to Palos
          Verdes.

                    ALICE
          I don't care what happens
          to him.
                    (beat)
          After the month I've spent in
          China, all I care about is
          having my family together.
          I don't want to see another
          airport...another passport.

Off-screen, a DOORBELL RINGS.

                    ALICE
          Now what?

Dave goes to answer the door and returns
with a large MAN in an ill-fitting suit.

                    BORIS
          I am Boris Yavitch from
          Moscow. Dr. Barron sent me.
            (reaches to kiss her hand)
          Madame Alice, such a
          privilege. I vant you should
          come to Russia with your
          balloons.

Alice's face slowly lights up with an
ominous smile.

                              FADE OUT:

UNDER THE TITLES

Alice and Dave are in bed, making love.
The TV is on the nightly news with no
sound.

Alice appears on the screen. It's the scene
from the airport.
Dave reaches for the remote control.

                    ALICE
          Honey, what's wrong?

                    DAVE
          Nothing, you're on television.
          Don't you want to hear?

She takes the remote from Dave and turns
off the TV.

                SCREEN GOES TO BLACK

www.ingramcontent.com/pod-product-compliance
Lightning Source LLC
LaVergne TN
LVHW050724240125
801953LV00001B/126